PERSUASION

In nineteenth-century England young women were expected to follow the advice of their families when choosing a husband, but Anne Elliot is not lucky in her family. Her mother is dead, and her father, Sir Walter Elliot, is a vain, silly man, who cares more about social rank than the happiness of his daughters. Anne's sister Elizabeth is cold and selfish, and her married sister Mary is always worrying about her imaginary illnesses and complaining about other people.

Only Lady Russell, a close friend of Anne's dead mother, has Anne's interests at heart. Persuasion from Lady Russell has a powerful effect on Anne when she is nineteen, and in love with a young naval officer with neither money nor social rank.

Eight years later Anne knows she made a mistake, and she wishes she had accepted Frederick Wentworth's offer of marriage. And when he returns, wealthy and successful, she realizes that her love for him is unchanged. But Captain Wentworth's love for her has clearly died, and Anne must hide the feelings in her heart . . .

9

9.

912.

(0:20-

OXFORD BOOKWORMS LIBRARY

Classics

Persuasion

Stage 4 (1400 headwords)

Series Editor: Jennifer Bassett
Founder Editor: Tricia Hedge
Activities Editors: Jennifer Bassett and Christine Lindop

JANE AUSTEN

Persuasion

Retold by
Clare West

OXFORD UNIVERSITY PRESS

OXFORD
UNIVERSITY PRESS

Great Clarendon Street, Oxford OX2 6DP

Oxford University Press is a department of the University of Oxford.
It furthers the University's objective of excellence in research, scholarship,
and education by publishing worldwide in

Oxford New York

Auckland Cape Town Dar es Salaam Hong Kong Karachi
Kuala Lumpur Madrid Melbourne Mexico City Nairobi
New Delhi Shanghai Taipei Toronto

With offices in

Argentina Austria Brazil Chile Czech Republic France Greece
Guatemala Hungary Italy Japan Poland Portugal Singapore
South Korea Switzerland Thailand Turkey Ukraine Vietnam

OXFORD and OXFORD ENGLISH are registered trade marks of
Oxford University Press in the UK and in certain other countries

This simplified edition © Oxford University Press 2008

Database right Oxford University Press (maker)

First published in Oxford Bookworms 2006

2 4 6 8 10 9 7 5 3 1

ISBN 978 0 19 479181 6

Printed in Hong Kong

ACKNOWLEDGEMENTS

The publishers would like to thank the following for permission to reproduce images:
photographs are from the BBC TV production *Persuasion*, and are reproduced courtesy
of BBC. The photos feature Susan Fleetwood, Amanda Root, Felicity Dean, Corin Redgrave,
Sophie Thompson, Emma Roberts, Victoria Hamilton, Ciarán Hinds, Phoebe Nicholls,
Samuel West, John Woodvine, Helen Schlesinger, and Jane Wood.

Word count (main text): 19,370 words

For more information on the Oxford Bookworms Library,
visit www.oup.com/elt/bookworms

CONTENTS

PEOPLE IN THIS STORY

Sir Walter Elliot, *a baronet, of Kellynch Hall*

Elizabeth Elliot

Anne Elliot } *Sir Walter's daughters*

Mary Musgrove

Charles Musgrove, *Mary's husband*

Louisa Musgrove } *Charles's sisters*

Henrietta Musgrove

Mr and Mrs Musgrove, *parents of Charles, Louisa, and Henrietta*

Charles Hayter, *a cousin of the Musgrove family*

Lady Russell, *a close friend of the Elliot family*

Mrs Clay, *Elizabeth Elliot's friend and companion*

William Elliot, *Sir Walter's cousin and heir*

Lady Dalrymple, *Sir Walter's cousin*

Mrs Smith, *a friend of Anne Elliot*

Mrs Rooke, *nurse to Mrs Smith*

Admiral Croft, *Sir Walter's tenant at Kellynch Hall*

Mrs Sophy Croft, *the Admiral's wife*

Captain Frederick Wentworth, *a naval officer, Mrs Croft's brother*

Edward Wentworth, *a vicar, Mrs Croft's brother*

Captain and Mrs Harville } *friends of Captain Wentworth*

Captain Benwick

A proud baronet

❧

 ir Walter Elliot, of Kellynch Hall, was a man who, for his
 own amusement, never opened any book except *The
Baronetage*. This was a history of all English baronets from
the very first to the most recent, and there Sir Walter passed
many a pleasant hour. There he could admire the long and
perfect blood-lines of the earliest baronets, and feel pity for
the new baronets of the last century. And there he could read
his own history with an interest which never failed – this
was the page at which the favourite book always fell open:

ELLIOT OF KELLYNCH HALL

Somerset, south-west England

Walter Elliot, born 1760, married Elizabeth Stevenson in
1784, by which lady (who died in 1800) he has three
children: Elizabeth, born 1785; Anne, born 1787; Mary,
born 1791 . . .

After Mary's name Sir Walter had added these words:

. . . married Charles, son and heir of Charles Musgrove
of Uppercross in Somerset, in 1810.

Two more pages described the rise of the family through the
centuries, with another note by Sir Walter at the end:

The heir to the baronetcy is Sir Walter Elliot's cousin, William Elliot.

Vanity was the beginning and the end of Sir Walter's character; vanity of person and of situation. He had been extremely handsome when young, and, at fifty-four, was still a very fine-looking man. Not many women could think more of their face and figure than he did. He considered beauty only a little less important than a baronetcy, and as he was fortunate enough to have both these good things, he kept his warmest admiration for himself.

It was probably his good looks and his baronetcy which had won him a wife of far better character than his own. Lady Elliot had been an excellent, sensible woman, whose only mistake was to fall in love with Sir Walter at the age of eighteen. For the next sixteen years she was not unhappy, however, and loved her children very much. Sadly, she fell ill, and as she lay dying, she worried about leaving her three daughters to the care of a vain, silly father. Fortunately, she had a very close friend, Lady Russell, who lived nearby, and who promised to help and advise the motherless girls.

Fourteen years had passed since Lady Elliot's death, and Lady Russell and Sir Walter were still neighbours. Lady Russell, whose husband had died much earlier, had not remarried. Neither had Sir Walter, who told his friends that he had decided to remain single because his daughters preferred it; he did not mention the one or two private disappointments he had had since his wife's death. Indeed, for one of his daughters he was prepared to do almost anything.

This was Elizabeth, his eldest, who was very handsome and very like himself. She and her father had the same interests and opinions, so were in agreement about most things, which was very pleasant for them both. Sir Walter's other two daughters were much less valuable to him. Mary had become a little more important now that she was a married lady, but Anne, with her intelligent mind and sweet nature, was of no importance at all to either father or sister. Her opinions were not listened to, her needs and wishes always came last – she was only Anne.

To Lady Russell, however, she was a most dear favourite and friend. Lady Russell loved them all, but it was only in Anne that she could see Lady Elliot come back to life.

A few years before, Anne had been a very pretty girl, but even then her father had not found anything to admire in her, because her pale skin and dark eyes were so different from his own. Now that she was older and thinner, he had no hope of ever reading of her marriage into one of the proud and ancient families in his favourite book. Mary, it was true, had found a husband, but the Musgroves were only a country family with money, not an ancient family like the Elliots. It was Elizabeth who Sir Walter depended on, to make the kind of marriage that would be suitable for a baronet's daughter.

It sometimes happens that a woman is handsomer at twenty-nine than she was ten years before, and it was so with Elizabeth. But seeing the years of danger coming closer, she did not feel quite as hopeful as her father. She did not enjoy reading *The Baronetage* any longer. When she opened it to see only her own birthday, followed by no marriage except her youngest sister's, she closed the book and pushed it away.

She had had a disappointment, too, which the book must always remind her of. When she was a very young girl, she had imagined that she would marry her father's heir, William Elliot. Her father had also wanted this to happen. William Elliot had not been known to them when he was a boy, but after Lady Elliot's death Sir Walter had written to him. And one spring, when Elizabeth was at her most beautiful, she had been introduced to the young man in London. She had found him very pleasant, and he was invited to Kellynch Hall. He was talked of and expected all the rest of the year, but he never came. The following spring he was again invited and expected, and again he did not come. The next piece of news was that he was married, to a woman of large fortune.

Sir Walter had been very angry. 'Why did he not ask my advice?' he repeated to anyone who would listen. 'I think I know best who he should marry. I am the head of the family, after all! And people have seen him with me. They will be surprised that a cousin of *mine* has married so low!'

But Mr Elliot never attempted to explain or apologize, and since then there had been no contact between Sir Walter and his heir.

Mr Elliot's rich wife died only a few years later, but Elizabeth was too proud to consider marrying him then. Kind friends had told her that he often spoke most rudely about the Elliots, so he could never be the right husband for Sir Walter's eldest daughter.

As well as disappointments about marriage, Elizabeth Elliot now had something else to worry about. Her father spent freely, but could not pay all the bills, and now owed money to a great number of people. In Sir Walter's opinion, a baronet had to live in a certain style; he was too proud to be careful. While Lady Elliot lived, she had helped to manage her husband's money, but since her death there had been no one to prevent Sir Walter from spending far too much.

He asked Elizabeth where he could make cuts in his spending. She could only suggest giving less money to the poor in the village, and not buying Anne her usual birthday present, but that would only save a very little.

The situation was clearly serious, so Sir Walter asked Lady Russell and his lawyer, Mr Shepherd, for their advice. Mr Shepherd was not brave enough to suggest any ideas himself, but felt sure that Lady Russell would have the right answer. Lady Russell herself thought long and hard about the problem, and even asked Anne's opinion, which no one else had considered worth doing. Together she and Anne wrote down a list of ways in which money could be saved.

'We must persuade your father to do all this,' Lady Russell said to Anne. 'If he does, in seven years he will be clear.'

Anne thought the plan was too gentle and that the money owed should be repaid more quickly, but she was used to following Lady Russell's advice, and agreed to the plan.

But when the list was shown to Sir Walter, it was received very badly.

'What! Shall I never be comfortable again?' he cried in horror. 'Journeys, London, servants, horses, wine – cuts in

'We must persuade your father to do all this,' said Lady Russell.

everything! To live no longer like a gentleman! No, I would prefer to leave Kellynch Hall at once than to remain here in conditions like these!'

'Leave Kellynch Hall.' The idea was immediately taken up by Mr Shepherd. 'Since you yourself have suggested it, Sir Walter,' he said smoothly, 'I do hope you will seriously consider it. Here you are well known for your style of living, in a fine, ancient house. Naturally, it is difficult to make cuts here. But in a different place, in a house which may be a little less grand, it would perhaps be easier to make changes.'

And after a few days of doubt and discussion, it was decided that Sir Walter and his daughters would move to Bath, a delightful city only fifty miles away. Sir Walter had at first thought of London, but Mr Shepherd, thinking that his employer would spend even more money there, had persuaded him to think again. All Anne's wishes had been for a smaller house near Kellynch, where they could occasionally revisit their old home. Lady Russell, however, thought her dear Anne was wrong in wanting to bury herself in the country; a change of air would do Anne good, and in a pleasantly busy place like Bath there would be every chance of finding interest and amusement, and of meeting new people who would admire her.

Lady Russell had another reason for wanting the family to move away to Bath. Elizabeth had recently become very close to a new friend, Mrs Clay. She was a daughter of Mr Shepherd, who had returned to her father's house with her two young children after a failed marriage. She was a clever young woman who understood very well how to please – at least, how to please Sir Walter. Lady Russell knew the baronet was a poor judge of character, and thought Mrs Clay was a most unsuitable friend for Elizabeth. She hoped the Elliots would see no more of her when they moved to Bath.

Mr Shepherd soon found a tenant for Kellynch Hall, but it was not easy to persuade Sir Walter that a naval man, even a high-ranking officer like an admiral, was the right person to live in a baronet's house.

'Who *is* this Admiral Croft?' asked Sir Walter coldly.

'A gentleman of excellent family, Sir Walter, with a very handsome fortune. He has long admired Kellynch Hall.'

'He fought in the battle of Trafalgar, I think,' added Anne.

'He is a married man without children,' continued Mr Shepherd, 'just what we would wish. A house needs a lady to take good care of it, and children, of course, can damage the furniture. I have met his wife – she is a very well-spoken, sensible lady. And what's more, Sir Walter, she is sister to a gentleman who lived near here, at Monkford, a few years ago – now, what was his name?'

'I have no idea, Shepherd. I can remember no gentleman living at Monkford.'

'Oh dear! I shall forget my own name next! What *was* his name?' He turned to his daughter, Mrs Clay. 'My dear, can you remember the name of the gentleman at Monkford, Mrs Croft's brother?'

But Mrs Clay was whispering and laughing so much with

Mrs Clay was a clever young woman who understood very well how to please Sir Walter.

Elizabeth that she did not even hear her father's question.

After waiting a moment, Anne said, 'You mean Mr Wentworth, I suppose.'

Mr Shepherd was very grateful. 'Wentworth! Thank you, Miss Elliot. Yes, that was his name. He was the vicar at Monkford. You remember him now, Sir Walter, I am sure.'

'Wentworth? Oh, Shepherd, you said a *gentleman*. I thought you were speaking of a man of rank and fortune. Mr Wentworth was a nobody – not worth remembering.'

Mr Shepherd saw at once it would be better not to mention Mr Wentworth again, but continued to describe the advantages of the Crofts – their age, and number, and fortune. Nothing, it seemed, would make them happier than renting Kellynch Hall from Sir Walter.

Sir Walter was finally persuaded to agree; in this his vanity played a large part. 'My tenant is Admiral Croft,' would sound extremely good, much better than 'My tenant is Mr—.' An admiral has his own importance, and, at the same time, can never make a baronet look small.

So it was decided, and Mr Shepherd was told to make the necessary arrangements. Anne, who had listened most carefully to the whole conversation, left the room and hurried out to the garden, to feel the cool air on her hot face. And as she walked along a favourite path, she whispered to herself:

'A few months more, and *he*, perhaps, will be walking here.'

2

A sad history

The man in Anne's anxious thoughts was not the Edward Wentworth who had been vicar of Monkford for several years, but his brother Frederick, a captain in the British navy. In the summer of 1806 Captain Wentworth had stayed with his brother in Monkford for six months. At that time he was a very fine young man, with plenty of intelligence and spirit, and Anne was an extremely pretty girl, with gentleness and feeling. They came to know each other well, and it was not at all surprising that they fell deeply in love.

A few days of perfect happiness followed, but soon there was trouble. When Sir Walter was asked for his agreement to the engagement, he did not actually refuse, but his great surprise and cold silences made it clear he thought it was a very poor marriage for his daughter.

And Lady Russell thought it would be a most unfortunate one.

'I should be very, very sad, Anne,' she had said, 'to see you married to a young man who has so uncertain a future, no friends to help him, and so little chance of success! No, no, it must not be! I have almost a mother's love for you, and I cannot watch Anne Elliot, the beautiful, intelligent daughter of a baronet, throw herself away at nineteen!'

Captain Wentworth had no fortune, but he was confident that he would soon have a ship to command and become rich. This confidence was very pleasing to Anne, but Lady Russell saw it differently. She saw carelessness, and danger, and these things filled her with horror.

Persuasion like this was too much for Anne to fight. Young and gentle as she was, she could not argue with both her father and Lady Russell, whose love and kindness to her had always been so great. So in the end she was persuaded to believe that the engagement was wrong, and with great difficulty and sadness she explained to Captain Wentworth that she could not marry him.

Their last meeting ended painfully. He thought she had behaved badly towards him, and he could not forgive her. Soon afterwards he went abroad.

Anne's sadness continued for many months, and as a result, she began to lose her prettiness and usual cheerfulness.

More than seven years had passed since this sad story came to its close, and time had by now softened much of her attachment to him. But no one ever came within the Kellynch circle who could be compared with Frederick Wentworth as she remembered him. When she was twenty-two, Charles Musgrove asked her to marry him; not long afterwards, he found a more willing mind in her younger sister. Lady Russell had been sorry that Anne had refused him, because the Musgroves were second in importance only to the Elliots in that part of Somerset, and because Charles himself was of good character. However, this time Anne had not asked for her friend's advice. And although Lady Russell never wished the past undone, she began now to lose hope that a suitable man would appear, to persuade Anne into marriage.

Neither Anne nor Lady Russell ever spoke of Captain Wentworth or of Anne's feelings for him, but Anne, at twenty-seven, thought very differently now.

'It was not Lady Russell's fault,' she told herself, 'or my own, for being guided by her, but I am sure I would be happier now, if I had kept to the engagement. If any young person asked *my* advice about an early attachment, I would certainly not persuade them against it.'

She also knew, from her reading of newspapers and navy lists, that Captain Wentworth had done what he hoped to do. He had made his fortune, and now commanded his own ship, and as far as she knew, he remained unmarried.

With all these feelings in her heart, it was painful to hear that his sister was going to live at Kellynch, but she was glad that the secret of her attachment was known only to her father, her sister Elizabeth, and Lady Russell. She hoped that no one else would ever learn of it.

In a few days' time Admiral and Mrs Croft were invited to Kellynch to discuss arrangements with Sir Walter and Mr Shepherd. The meeting was highly successful.

Afterwards Sir Walter said to his eldest daughter, 'I must say, Elizabeth, the Admiral is the best-looking sailor I have ever met. If only I could lend him my man-servant to do his hair, I would not be ashamed to go out with him anywhere!'

And the Admiral said to his wife, as they drove away, 'You see, my dear, the baronet will never set the world on fire, but there's no harm in him!'

It was agreed the Crofts would move into the house in October, and Sir Walter would move to Bath the month before. Anne did not look forward to spending a hot September in the city rather than the countryside, but felt it was her duty to go with her father and sister.

Luckily, however, something else happened which gave her a different duty. Her younger sister Mary, who often imagined herself to be ill and who always wanted Anne as her nurse, suddenly decided she was unwell again.

'I need Anne at Uppercross Cottage,' she told Elizabeth. 'Only Anne knows how to take care of me when I'm like this.'

And Elizabeth's reply was, 'Then I'm sure Anne had better stay with you, because nobody will need her in Bath.'

Anne, glad to feel useful, happily agreed to Mary's request, or rather, command. And so it was decided that Anne would stay in Uppercross and not go to Bath until Lady Russell could take her there, after Christmas.

So far all the plans were going well, except for one thing – Mrs Clay had been invited to live with the Elliots in Bath, as Elizabeth's dearest companion and friend. Anne knew more than she wished to know of her father's character, and she was fearful of the possible effects on him of this closeness. Although Mrs Clay had freckles and thick wrists and ankles, she was young, with a pretty face, a sharp mind, and pleasing ways. These last two were by far the greatest danger, Anne thought. She decided to warn her sister, although she had little hope of success.

Elizabeth was angry. 'Mrs Clay never forgets her situation in life, and I think I know her rather better than you do. Nor do I think we need suspect my father now – he has kept himself single all this time because of us. If she were very beautiful, perhaps it would be wrong to have her with me so much. But the poor woman's freckles! I have heard my father say how ugly they are, a thousand times!'

'A pleasant manner,' said Anne, 'can nearly always make people forget any little ugliness in the face.'

'I think very differently,' Elizabeth replied coldly. 'A pleasant manner goes well with a handsome face, but can never change an ugly one. And as the eldest, I have much more to lose than you, so I think it rather unnecessary for you to give me this advice.'

Anne said no more, but was not completely without hope that her warning would have some effect.

Soon the day for leaving Kellynch arrived, and Sir Walter, Elizabeth, and Mrs Clay drove off to their new life in Bath. With her mind full of sad thoughts, Anne walked the short distance to Lady Russell's home, and later that day Lady Russell drove her the few miles to Uppercross Cottage.

The village of Uppercross contained workers' houses, the vicar's house, and the Great House, where Mr and Mrs Musgrove lived with their two daughters. When their son Charles married Mary Elliot, they rebuilt an old farmhouse into something much grander, called it Uppercross Cottage, and gave it to him and his young wife to live in.

Anne had often stayed here. She knew the ways of Uppercross as well as those of Kellynch. The two Musgrove families were so much in the habit of running in and out of each other's houses at all hours that it was rather a surprise for Anne to find Mary alone.

However, finding Mary unwell and miserable was quite usual. When Anne came into the sitting room, Mary was lying down, feeling very sorry for herself.

Mary was lying down, feeling very sorry for herself.

A sad history

'So, you are here at last!' she said. 'I began to think I would never see you. I am so ill, I can only just speak. I have not seen anybody, not a single person, all morning!'

'I'm sorry to find you ill,' said Anne. 'How is Charles?'

'Oh, he is out shooting, though I told him how ill I was.'

'You have your little boys with you?'

'Yes, but they're so noisy that they do me more harm than good. They're quite unmanageable!'

'Well, you'll soon be better now,' said Anne brightly. 'You know I always make you better when I come to stay. How are your neighbours at the Great House?'

'Oh, I cannot tell you! I have not seen one of them today, except Mr Musgrove, who just stopped and spoke through the window, but without getting off his horse. I told him how ill I was, but not one of them has been to visit me.'

'I expect you will see the Miss Musgroves later.'

'Oh, I never want to see *them*. They talk and laugh far too much for me. Oh Anne, I am so very unwell! It was quite unkind of you not to come last week.'

'My dear Mary, remember what you wrote to me. You said you were perfectly well. And I have been so busy that I could not very easily leave Kellynch sooner.'

'Dear me! What can *you* possibly have to do?'

'A great many things.' And Anne started describing the organizing and packing she had been doing, only to stop when she realized Mary was no longer listening.

After a little more cheerful conversation, Mary soon began to feel better. Anne persuaded her to eat something, and then

17

her sister was well enough to suggest taking a little walk. They went to the Great House to call on the Musgroves, where they were given a warm welcome by the family.

Mr and Mrs Musgrove were very good-hearted, honest, friendly people, who lived in the old English style, and liked everything around them to be comfortable. Their daughters Henrietta and Louisa, aged nineteen and twenty, had more modern ideas, and, like many other young ladies, wished only to be fashionable and enjoy themselves. They dressed well, they had pretty faces and good manners; they were popular with everyone. Anne thought they were two of the happiest people she knew. She herself preferred the calm enjoyment of books and reading to dancing and parties, but she often wished that she had, with her own sisters, the same perfect understanding and fond attachment which there was between the Musgrove sisters.

Anne knew that she would enjoy her two months at Uppercross. The cottage itself was comfortable, Mary was pleasanter to her than Elizabeth was, and she got on well with Mary's husband and children. Charles was a pleasant, cheerful man, who enjoyed his sport and his shooting, and did little else. There was very often a little disagreement between him and Mary, but for most of the time it was thought – if no one looked too closely – that they were a happy couple.

A less enjoyable part of staying at Uppercross for Anne, however, was that everybody always came to her with their difficulties, which were very often about her sister Mary.

Charles would come to her and say quietly, 'I wish you

The Musgrove girls, Louisa and Henrietta, were popular with everyone.

could persuade Mary to stop always imagining herself to be ill all the time . . .'

And Mary, when she was feeling unhappy, would say to Anne, 'I do believe that if Charles saw me dying, he would not think there was anything wrong with me. Please, Anne, try to persuade him that I really am very ill . . .'

The two little boys also seemed to be a problem. Mrs Musgrove to Anne:

'My grandsons are fine boys, but oh, what trouble they are! You're so sensible yourself, Anne – can't you try to give your sister a little advice about how to manage her children . . .'

Mary saw things differently. 'I hate sending the boys to their grandmother. She's always giving them sweets and cakes, and then they are sick and cross for the rest of the day . . .'

Louisa also wanted Anne's help with Mary. 'Could you persuade Mary not to be so proud? Everyone knows she's a baronet's daughter and so a higher social rank than Mama, but it would be so much more pleasant if she didn't push herself to the front *all* the time. Mama doesn't mind, but everyone notices . . .'

How was Anne to find the answers to all these problems? She listened patiently, offered explanations, and gave gentle advice, and to her sister, sometimes rather stronger advice.

A month passed, and Anne heard that the Crofts had moved into Kellynch. Charles and Mary went to visit them, and the next day the visit was returned. Anne was glad to be there, because she wished to meet Captain Wentworth's sister.

She found Mrs Croft a sensible, open-minded lady, who seemed to have no idea of Anne's attachment to the Captain. During their conversation, however, Mrs Croft said, 'You knew my brother, I believe, when he was living in Somerset. Perhaps you have not heard that he is married?'

Anne, her mind jumping at once to Frederick, tried desperately to control her feelings, but in a few seconds it became clear that Mrs Croft was talking about her *other* brother, Edward, who had been the vicar at Monkton.

Calmness returned to Anne's heart, until, just as the Crofts were leaving, she heard the Admiral say to Mary, 'We're expecting one of my wife's brothers here soon.'

Anne was left anxiously wondering *which* brother, but later that day she heard from Louisa Musgrove that it was in fact Captain Wentworth who was expected, and that Mr and Mrs Musgrove were greatly looking forward to meeting him. Their younger son Richard, a worthless, useless boy, had joined the navy and spent six months on Captain Wentworth's ship. When he died abroad, his loving parents forgot all his faults and remembered him as a favourite child. In his letters home, he had told his family how kind the Captain had been to him. Now they could not stop talking about the great Captain Wentworth, whom poor Richard had so much admired.

It was difficult for Anne to listen to all this talk of the fine young officer who would soon be among them, but she knew she must teach herself to hear his name, see his face, and even talk to him, without showing her true feelings in any way.

3

The return of Captain Wentworth

❧

A few days more, and Captain Wentworth was known to be at Kellynch. Anne knew she must be calm, because soon they would meet. And on the day when he paid his first visit to the Musgroves at the Great House, Anne and Mary were also planning to call there. But just as they were leaving the cottage, Mary's elder boy was brought home after a bad fall while playing outside. The child was in great pain, and there were fears that he had injured his back.

The visit to the Great House was forgotten at once. Anne had to do everything – send for the doctor, send someone to inform the absent father, calm the screaming mother, and take care of the poor injured child. Fortunately the doctor arrived quickly.

'No bones are broken, I think,' he said. 'But we will keep a careful eye on the boy. We must hope for the best.'

Later in the afternoon, when the house was calm again, Henrietta and Louisa arrived, to tell Anne and Mary about Captain Wentworth's visit. They were perfectly delighted with him. How handsome he was! Such pleasant manners! He was far more agreeable than any other man they knew.

'He is a perfect gentleman!' cried Henrietta. 'We are both quite in love with him already, I promise you!'

'We are both quite in love with him already!' cried Henrietta.

'And can you believe it,' added Louisa, 'he is coming to dinner tomorrow!'

In the evening Mr and Mrs Musgrove also came to the cottage, to find out how their grandson was, and to talk about the Captain's visit.

'I'm sorry, Charles,' said his father kindly, 'that you and Mary probably will not be able to come to dinner tomorrow, to meet Captain Wentworth. You won't want to leave the little boy.'

'Oh no! We could not possibly leave him when he's in such pain!' cried Mary wildly.

'Perhaps I could go for just half an hour,' suggested her husband.

'Oh no, Charles, I won't hear of it! You must stay here!'

But the following afternoon, when the child had had a quiet day, and the doctor had visited a second time, Charles decided he would not be needed at home that evening.

'My father very much wishes me to meet the Captain, my love,' he told Mary, 'so I shall go to dinner at the Great House. You would not like to leave the boy yourself, but you see *I* can be of no use. And you have your sister with you.'

Mary knew from Charles's voice that he was determined to go, so she said nothing until he was out of the room.

'So! You and I, Anne, will be left here alone, with this poor sick child – and no one will come near us all evening! This is always my luck! If there is anything unpleasant going on, men are always sure to get out of it. And I am really not well enough to look after a sick child.'

'Well, if you wish to go,' said Anne, 'perhaps you should. Leave the boy to my care. I will stay here to be with him.'

'Are you serious?' cried Mary, her eyes brightening. 'That's a very good thought, an excellent thought, Anne! And you are so good with him. There's no need for me to be here too.'

And so it was decided. Anne was quite happy to see them go off cheerfully together to the Great House. She knew she could be of use to the sick child, and what was it to her, if Frederick Wentworth were only half a mile away, being pleasant and amusing with other people!

'How does he feel about meeting me?' she wondered. 'Why has he waited all this time to see me again? Why didn't he return to ask for my hand in marriage, as soon as he became rich and successful? I suppose the answer must be because he no longer wished to marry me.'

The next morning Anne and Mary were just starting breakfast when Charles came in to say that he was going shooting with Captain Wentworth, that his sisters were outside with the Captain, and that the Captain would like to come in to say good morning. Mary was delighted at the news of this unexpected little visit, but a thousand different feelings ran through Anne's mind in a second. Her one clear thought was that it would soon be over.

And it was soon over. He was in the room; her eyes met his; she heard his voice; he talked to Mary; he spoke to the Miss Musgroves, laughed with them like old friends. The room seemed full – full of persons and voices – but a few minutes ended it. Their visitor said goodbye and left with

Charles and his sisters. The room was cleared, and Anne was left to finish her breakfast, if she could.

'It is over! It is over!' she repeated to herself gratefully. 'The worst is over, now I have seen him again!'

Mary talked, but Anne did not listen. She had seen him. They had met. They had been once more in the same room!

Soon, however, she tried to think sensibly, and to control her feelings. How silly to return to the heartache and pain of almost eight years ago! But was there any way of reading his feelings? Did he seem to want to avoid her? And the next moment she was hating herself for asking the question.

One other question, which she could not put out of her mind, was soon answered. Mary passed on some information she had been given by Henrietta.

'Captain Wentworth is not very polite about you, Anne. When Henrietta asked him what he thought of you, he said you had changed so much that he had difficulty recognizing you. But he appeared to greatly enjoy talking to *me*.'

'Changed so much!' thought Anne, deeply hurt and ashamed. Doubtless it was so, and she could take no revenge, because he looked no older. No, the years which had destroyed her beauty had only given him a more manly look.

Frederick Wentworth had no idea that his words would reach Anne's ears. He had not forgiven her. She had behaved badly to him and disappointed him; worse, she had shown weakness of character. She had given in to the persuasion of her friends and family.

26

He had been most warmly attached to her, and had never seen a woman since whom he could compare with her. But he had no wish to meet her again. Her power over him was gone for ever.

Now he planned to marry, and he was actually looking round, ready to fall in love. He had a heart for either of the Miss Musgroves, if they could catch it; a heart, in short, for any pleasing young woman, except Anne Elliot.

'Any woman between fifteen and thirty,' he laughingly told his sister, Mrs Croft, 'may have me as a husband. A little beauty, a few smiles, and I am a lost man.' But his bright, proud eye showed that he wanted much more than that. He added, 'She must have a strong mind, and sweetness of nature – that is the woman I want.' Anne Elliot was not far from his thoughts as he spoke.

From this time Captain Wentworth and Anne Elliot were repeatedly in the same social circle. They soon met at dinner at the Great House, and other meetings quickly followed. They had no conversation together except what was needed for politeness. Once so much to each other! Now nothing! There *had* been a time when they had wanted to talk only to each other, and had so many ideas and feelings to talk about. But now they were strangers.

At these family parties, there was a very great interest in ships and the navy. The Miss Musgroves, who seemed to have eyes only for the Captain, were full of questions.

'Oh, Captain Wentworth, do tell us some more about your first ship, the *Asp*. Was she a very fine ship?'

'Not at all,' said the Captain, amused. 'She was old, and full of holes. But she and I were lucky. There was a storm once near Gibraltar, just after we'd had a battle with a French ship that I was chasing . . .'

Listening to these stories of storms and battles, the Miss Musgroves would scream in anxious horror at the danger the Captain had been in. Anne too had these feelings, but kept them to herself.

The evenings often ended with dancing. Anne always offered to play the piano, and although her eyes sometimes filled with tears as she sat there, she was extremely glad to be doing something useful, and was happy not to be noticed.

No one seemed more cheerful than the Captain. Mr and Mrs Musgrove considered him a true friend, because he had helped their poor son Richard, and the young women all admired him. Henrietta and Louisa appeared to think of nothing else but him, and their cousins, the Miss Hayters, who often came to join in the dancing, also seemed to be in love with him.

Once Anne felt that he was looking at her – noticing her changed face, perhaps – and *once* she heard him ask Louisa, 'Doesn't Miss Elliot ever dance?'

The answer was, 'Oh no, never! She prefers to play – she is never tired of playing the piano.'

Once, too, he spoke to her. On her return to the piano, which she had left for a moment, she found him sitting there. He got up at once, saying,

'I am so sorry, madam, this is your seat.'

Anne always offered to play the piano, and was glad
to be doing something useful.

Anne did not wish for more looks or words like these. His cold politeness was worse than anything.

Captain Wentworth had planned to stay only a short time at Kellynch, but he soon changed his plans. At Uppercross the old people were so friendly and the young so agreeable that he decided to stay longer. Now he visited Uppercross every day, and often went shooting with Charles.

Up to now the only opinion of Captain Wentworth,

among the Musgroves and Hayters, had been one of warm admiration. But when a certain Charles Hayter returned from a short holiday, and found the Captain so much a part of his family circle, he felt very differently. Charles Hayter was the eldest of all the cousins, a very pleasing young man, who was studying to be a vicar. There had been a strong attachment between him and Henrietta, but on his return, he found the lady far less interested in him than in Captain Wentworth.

At Uppercross Cottage there was much discussion of this.

'It would be a good thing if Henrietta married the Captain,' said Mary. 'So much better than throwing herself away on Charles Hayter, who is nothing – just a nobody!'

'Don't be silly, Mary,' said her husband. 'Charles Hayter is an excellent young man. If he marries Henrietta, and Captain Wentworth marries Louisa, I shall be very well pleased.'

'Lousia?' cried Mary. 'Oh no, the Captain likes Henrietta best, I'm sure of it.'

'It would be a very good marriage for either of my sisters,' Charles said. 'I've never seen a pleasanter man in my life than the Captain. I believe he made a fortune of twenty thousand pounds in the war.'

Anne could only listen, with pain in her heart.

One morning Captain Wentworth walked into the sitting room at the cottage. Only Anne and the injured boy were in the room, and the Captain seemed uncomfortable at finding himself almost alone with Anne.

'I am sorry – I thought the Miss Musgroves were here,' he said, and walked to the window to give himself time to think.

'They are upstairs with my sister,' replied Anne, trying to remain calm. 'They will come down soon.'

'I hope the little boy is better,' said the Captain politely, and was silent. Then the door opened again, and Charles Hayter entered. He seemed unwilling to make conversation with the Captain, and sat down to read a newspaper.

A minute later Mary's younger son Walter, who was two years old, ran into the room. He wanted to play with his sick brother, but when Anne told him not to, he climbed on her back and started pulling her hair.

'Walter,' said Anne, 'get down this moment!'

'Walter,' cried Charles Hayter, 'do as you are told! Don't you hear your aunt? Come to me, come to cousin Charles!'

But Walter did not move.

In another moment Anne was free of him. Someone unfastened his little hands from around her neck and took him away. That someone was Captain Wentworth.

Anne could not speak; she could not even thank him. His kindness in stepping forward to help her, his cold politeness while doing it, produced such confused feelings in her that she had to leave the room at once. She was ashamed of herself for being so sensitive over such a small thing, but it was some time before she was able to talk and behave normally again.

4

A trip to Lyme

Anne soon had her own opinions about the feelings that the four young people had for each other. Louisa seemed to be Captain Wentworth's favourite, but Anne did not think he was in love with either of the sisters; they were more in love with him. Poor Charles Hayter seemed very disappointed, although Henrietta still showed a little interest in him from time to time. Anne wished she could show them what a dangerous game they were all playing, and the unhappiness it could lead to. She knew that none of them meant to hurt each other, especially Captain Wentworth, who, she felt sure, had no idea of Charles's feelings for Henrietta. But she did think it was wrong of him to accept the admiration of two young women at the same time.

After a few days, however, Charles Hayter appeared to recognize defeat, and he no longer came to Uppercross. Mary hoped that Henrietta had sent him away, and her husband hoped every day to see him return. Anne could only feel that it was sensible of Charles Hayter to keep away.

One fine November morning, the Miss Musgroves came to the cottage to ask if Mary and Anne would like to go on a walk with them. Just as the four young women were leaving the cottage, Charles Musgrove and the Captain returned from shooting, and were invited to join them. Anne now wished she had remained at home, but during the walk she was careful to stay close to Mary and Charles, leaving Captain Wentworth to walk with the Musgrove sisters.

She tried hard to keep her mind busy, with thoughts of her favourite books, or admiration for the fine views over the autumn fields, but she could not help hearing some of the conversation between the Captain and Louisa.

'What wonderful weather for the Admiral and my sister!' said the Captain. 'They are out driving their carriage today. I wonder where he will overturn it this time? It happens very often, I can tell you. But my sister thinks nothing of it.'

'I would feel just the same in her place!' cried Louisa enthusiastically. 'If I loved a man, as she loves the Admiral, nothing should ever separate us! I would prefer an accident with him to a safe journey with anyone else!'

'Would you?' he cried warmly. 'How right you are!' And there was silence between them for a moment.

The view over the fields, Anne decided, was no longer so attractive; the autumn colours were sad and grey. Soon, however, the walkers turned on to another path, and saw below them a low, rather ugly farmhouse. This was Winthrop, where the Hayter family lived.

'Oh!' said Mary, 'is that Winthrop? I had no idea we had come so far. We must turn back at once. Come, Henrietta!'

Henrietta blushed, and seemed ashamed.

'No, no!' cried Louisa, taking her sister's arm. 'We must visit our cousins, now we are here.'

'We must turn back at once,' said Mary. 'Come, Henrietta!'

Charles too wished to visit his cousins, but Mary was determined not to set foot in the house. After a little heated discussion between the sisters, it was decided that Charles and Henrietta would make a quick visit to the Hayters, while the rest of the group waited for them on the hill.

Louisa and the Captain walked around together, and Anne found a sunny place for Mary to sit down, with her back against a hedge. While Mary was busy making herself comfortable, Anne suddenly heard Louisa's clear voice on the other side of the hedge.

'And so I *made* Henrietta go,' Louisa was saying. 'It is her dearest wish to see Charles, I am sure! And Mary very nearly persuaded her not to go. Can you believe it? I would never be so easily persuaded!'

'Lucky for her, to have such a mind as yours to guide her!' replied the Captain. 'Your sister is a lovely woman, but *you* have all the spirit. What damage weakness of character can cause! My first wish for all my friends is that they should be firm. If you hope for happiness all your life, Louisa, you must keep your present firmness of character!'

There was a pause. Anne wondered how Louisa could possibly answer words of such interest, spoken so warmly.

'Mary has too much of the Elliot pride,' said Louisa, after a while. 'The Hayter connection is not good enough for her. We all wish brother Charles had married Anne instead – he asked her first, you know, before Mary.'

'Do you mean, Anne refused him?' asked the Captain after a short pause. 'When did that happen?'

'Oh, about a year before he married Mary – in 1809, I think. I was still at school. We all like Anne much more than Mary. But mother and father think Anne's great friend Lady Russell persuaded her to refuse Charles.'

They moved on, and Anne heard no more, but what she had heard was very painful to her. She saw what Captain Wentworth thought of her own character; and his questions about her showed an interest that made her heart beat faster.

When Charles and Henrietta returned, they brought Charles Hayter with them. There now seemed to be a perfect understanding between Henrietta and Charles Hayter, and both looked extremely happy.

Everything now marked out Louisa for Captain Wentworth. And as the group walked slowly home, Louisa walked alone with the Captain, talking enthusiastically, while he listened seriously, his eyes on her pretty face.

Soon the footpath crossed a road, and they saw a carriage coming along. It was the Admiral and Mrs Croft on their way home. They stopped and offered to take with them any of the ladies who were tired. The invitation was generally refused, but as the carriage was about to leave, Captain Wentworth quickly whispered something to his sister.

'Miss Elliot,' Mrs Croft said to Anne at once, 'I am sure you are tired. Do let us take you home.'

The Admiral added some kind words to his wife's, and Anne was not allowed to refuse. In a moment she felt the Captain's hand under her elbow, helping her into the carriage.

Yes, she was in the carriage, and he had placed her there with his own hands. He had seen how tired she was and been determined to help her. She understood him. He could not forgive her for the past, but he could not be unfeeling. What a warm, true heart he had! And this was the man she had refused to marry!

As she travelled home in the carriage, she was only half listening to the Crofts' conversation. They were wondering which of the Musgrove girls Frederick would choose for his wife, but Anne kept her opinions to herself.

The trip to Lyme, a town about twenty miles away, happened a few days later. Captain Wentworth had been to visit a good friend of his, Captain Harville, who was living in Lyme with his family, and on his return he described the town and the seaside around with great enthusiasm. At once the young people of Uppercross were wild to see Lyme themselves, and Louisa was so eager that she would hear no arguments against the idea. And so to Lyme they went – Charles, Mary, Anne, Henrietta, Louisa, and Captain Wentworth.

The plan was to drive down in two carriages, see the sights, meet the Captain's friends, and return the following day. When they arrived, they found rooms at an inn, and went out to visit the ancient town, delighted with its beautiful situation right on the sea. They walked first along the beach, and then came to the Cobb, the famous harbour wall. Every visitor to Lyme must climb the steps and walk along the Cobb, to admire the views over the sea and along the beautiful line of cliffs to the east of the town.

After their walk the young people were introduced to Captain Harville and his wife, and found them very pleasant and friendly. Staying with the Harvilles was another friend, Captain Benwick, a quiet, serious person. He had been engaged to marry Captain Harville's sister Fanny, who had died some months ago. Poor Benwick, Captain Wentworth had told his Uppercross friends, had been very deeply attached to Fanny Harville, and seemed unable to recover from the pain of losing her.

'And yet,' thought Anne, 'he has not, perhaps, a sadder

37

Every visitor to Lyme must climb the steps and walk along the Cobb.

heart than I have. I cannot believe his future is without hope.
As a man, he has more chances to start again than I have. He
will recover from this, and be happy with someone else.'

That evening at the Harvilles' house, Anne found herself
at Captain Benwick's side, and was soon in a deep discussion
with him about books. The young man was very fond of
writers who talked about the pains of love, the misery of a
broken heart, and Anne tried gently to suggest other books
to him, which might help him to be stronger, and to turn his
mind away from his own suffering. Captain Benwick listened
carefully, and seemed grateful for the interest she took in him.

The next morning the ladies went for an early walk by the

sea with Captain Wentworth. As they came up the steps from the beach, a gentleman stood back to let them pass. Anne's face caught his eye, and he looked at her with great admiration. She was looking very well; the sea air had given colour and freshness to her skin and brightness to her eyes.

Captain Wentworth noticed the gentleman's admiring stare, and gave Anne a quick look, which seemed to say, 'That man admires you – and even *I*, at this moment, see something like the old Anne Elliot again.'

Soon the walkers returned to the inn for breakfast, and as they entered, they saw the same gentleman again, who was just getting into his carriage to leave. And for a second time, the young man looked admiringly at Anne.

At breakfast Captain Wentworth asked one of the inn servants if he knew who the gentleman was.

'Yes, sir, a Mr Elliot, Mr William Elliot. A very rich young gentleman, sir, on his way to Bath.'

'Mr Elliot!' cried Mary, in great excitement. 'It must be our cousin, our father's heir! Anne, Charles, it must be, mustn't it? Oh, what a pity we were not introduced to him!'

Anne quietly reminded her that their father and William Elliot had not spoken to each other for years. Secretly, however, Anne was pleased that her father's heir was undoubtedly a gentleman.

Later, there was a second walk by the sea, this time along the Cobb. It became too windy for the ladies on the higher wall, so they agreed to go down to the lower path. Everyone climbed down the steep steps carefully, except Louisa, who was determined to jump. She wanted Captain Wentworth to catch her, as he had often done before on their walks at Uppercross when she jumped down from low field walls. The Captain advised her against it, thought the pavement too hard for jumping, but no, she would not listen. She smiled at him and said firmly, 'I am determined to do it!'

He put out his hands; she jumped too soon by half a second; she fell on the pavement on the Lower Cobb, and lay there, lifeless!

There was no wound, no blood; but her eyes were closed, she did not appear to breathe, her face was like death. The horror of that moment to all who stood around!

The horror of that moment to all who stood around!

Captain Wentworth knelt down beside Louisa, his face as white as her own. Anne also hurried to Louisa's side.

'She is dead! She is dead!' screamed Mary, and fell back, into her husband's arms. Henrietta too was helpless with shock and terror.

'Oh God!' cried Captain Wentworth wildly. 'Her father and mother!'

'A doctor!' said Anne. 'We must fetch a doctor.'

He caught the word, and jumped up to go in search of one, when Anne said, 'It would be better for Captain Benwick to go – he knows Lyme and will find a doctor more easily.'

Everyone saw how sensible this was, and at once Captain Benwick ran off into town.

'Anne, Anne,' cried Charles, who was taking care of his wife, 'what is to be done next?' Captain Wentworth's eyes also turned towards her, silently asking for her help.

'I think we should carry her gently to the inn,' said Anne.

'Yes – yes, I am sure. Carry her to the inn.'

'To the inn, yes,' repeated Wentworth, more calmly now. 'I will carry her myself.'

As they left the Cobb, they met the Harvilles, who, hearing the terrible news from Captain Benwick, had come to offer their home and everything they had, to help poor Louisa. Their offer was gratefully accepted, and Louisa was carried to their house.

The doctor was soon with them – and his report gave them all hope. No bones were broken; the only injury was to her head, but he had seen people recover from worse injuries;

41

he was not without hope; he spoke cheerfully. Anne would never forget Captain Wentworth's heartfelt cry of 'Thank God!' as he heard the doctor's words.

The Harvilles were determined to keep Louisa under their roof until she was fit enough to travel; Mrs Harville was an experienced nurse, who promised to take care of the patient, and watch over her, night and day.

The next step was to inform Louisa's parents. It was decided that Charles would stay by his sister's side in Lyme for the next few days, while Captain Wentworth took the ladies back to Uppercross.

'But if Anne would stay,' suggested Captain Wentworth, 'to help Mrs Harville – there is no one so suitable, so responsible as Anne!'

And so it was agreed. Anne was happy to stay, and it gave her a warm feeling to know that the Captain thought so well of her. But when Mary heard about the plan, the peace came to a sudden end.

'Why should Anne stay, instead of me? Am I not just as useful as Anne? Why am I expected to go away? Louisa is *my* sister-in-law, not Anne's. And to go home without my husband! No, it is too unkind!'

In short, Mary was determined to stay, and neither Charles nor anybody else could fight against it. So Anne found herself in the carriage with Henrietta and Captain Wentworth, on their way back to Uppercross.

At first, Henrietta could not stop crying, but after a while she cried herself to sleep in a corner of the carriage. Captain

Wentworth, though silent for much of the time, could not always keep his feelings under control.

'Oh God!' he cried once. 'I wish I had not allowed her to jump! I wish I had stopped her. Dear, sweet Louisa! So determined! Such spirit!'

Anne wondered if he still considered firmness the key to happiness in life, but with her usual gentleness she tried to calm him.

The journey went quickly, and when they arrived at the Great House, Captain Wentworth went in alone to tell the Musgroves the terrible news. As soon as he had done so, and seen Henrietta and Anne safely received by the family, he returned immediately to Lyme.

5

Arrival in Bath

❧

Anne spent two days with the Musgroves at the Great House, before going to stay with Lady Russell at Kellynch. She made herself very useful, and helped them to make arrangements for the future; the poor parents were too worried and miserable to think for themselves.

Charles came up from Lyme, bringing news that Louisa's condition was more or less the same. However, the doctor was sure, Charles said, that she would recover completely in time. They were all very grateful to the Harvilles, especially Mrs Harville, who was such an excellent nurse.

Charles returned to Lyme the same day, taking with him an old family servant to help with the nursing. His parents were unhappy to see him go, and even more unhappy when they realized their dear Anne was leaving Uppercross the following day for Kellynch.

'What shall we do without you?' cried poor Mrs Musgrove.

Anne found it easy to persuade them. 'I think you should both go to Lyme,' she said. 'You will feel so much better, and more cheerful, when you can see Louisa for yourselves.'

'You're always right, dear Anne!' said Mrs Musgrove. 'And we can be useful, and take care of Mrs Harville's children while she is with Louisa. Yes, we'll go tomorrow!'

When Anne waved goodbye to them the next morning, she felt pleased with what she had done, but there was sadness in her heart as she looked round the Great House before leaving it herself. She knew very well what would follow Louisa's recovery. In a few months' time these quiet, empty rooms would be filled with all that was happy and loving, all that was most unlike Anne Elliot!

An hour later Lady Russell's carriage arrived to collect Anne. Lady Russell was delighted to see her dear Anne again, but was also a little anxious, because she knew who had been a frequent visitor to Uppercross in recent weeks.

Anne found it difficult to mention Captain Wentworth's name to Lady Russell, but it was necessary to describe the accident at Lyme and also explain the attachment between the Captain and Louisa.

Lady Russell listened calmly, and hoped they would be very happy, but secretly she was angry. To think that a man who at twenty-three seemed to value Anne Elliot should, eight years later, fall in love with a silly girl like Louisa Musgrove!

Three days afterwards, Lady Russell and Anne went to visit Admiral and Mrs Croft at Kellynch Hall. Anne discovered that Captain Wentworth had been there the day before, had stayed only a few hours and then returned to Lyme.

'He asked about your health, dear Miss Elliot,' said Mrs Croft, 'and hoped very much that you were well. He was so grateful to you for all you did when that terrible accident happened. He spoke about it several times.'

These kind words gave Anne great happiness. There was,

however, no danger of meeting Captain Wentworth at Kellynch, as the Crofts were going away for a few weeks, while Lady Russell and Anne were moving to Bath.

Soon Charles and Mary came to visit Anne at Lady Russell's house. They each had different things to talk about.

'Louisa can sit up in bed now,' said Charles. 'But my parents do not feel she will be well enough to come home for the Christmas holidays.'

'We had so much to do in Lyme!' said his wife. 'Dinner and walks with the Harvilles, borrowing books from the library and then returning them, meeting the Harvilles' friends, going to the shops – Lyme is far more interesting than Uppercross!'

'And how is Captain Benwick?' asked Anne.

Mary looked annoyed. 'Oh, very well, but he's a strange young man! We invited him to Uppercross, and he was quite delighted. Then suddenly he changed his mind and said it had all been a mistake. I cannot understand why. Uppercross is pleasant enough for a heartbroken man like him, surely!'

Charles laughed and said, 'Now, Mary, you know very well how it was.' He turned to Anne. 'It was all your fault. He thought he would find *you* there if he came to see us. When he discovered Lady Russell lived three miles away, it was a great disappointment to him. He admires you very much, you know.'

'Oh Charles, really!' said Mary. 'I never heard him mention Anne twice all the time I was there.'

'You weren't listening to him, Mary. His head is full of

some books that you advised him to read, Anne, and he wants to discuss them with you. Miss Elliot's sweetness, her beauty, her fine mind – that's what I heard him say, again and again.'

'Well!' said Mary crossly. 'The woman he was engaged to, poor Fanny Harville, only died last June! Such a heart is not worth having – don't you agree, Lady Russell?'

'I must see him before I decide,' smiled Lady Russell.

'I am sure he will come and visit you,' said Charles. 'I explained how to get here, and he listened with great interest.'

'You will not like him, Lady Russell,' said Mary. 'He sits all day reading his book, and does not notice if a person makes conversation or drops her scissors or anything like that.'

Lady Russell laughed. And for the next week both she and Anne, without mentioning it to each other, looked forward to Captain Benwick's visit. But he did not come. Perhaps he was less enthusiastic about seeing Anne than Charles had imagined, or he was too shy. In the end Lady Russell decided he was not worth the interest she had begun to take in him.

Soon it was time for Lady Russell to take Anne to Bath. As they drove into the city in Lady Russell's carriage on a wet afternoon, Anne could not pretend to be cheerful. She saw the narrowness of the crowded streets and heard the noisy cries of the cake-sellers. She had never liked Bath and was in no hurry to arrive, because who would welcome her arrival?

She had recently received a letter from her sister Elizabeth,

informing her that Mr William Elliot was in Bath. He had
visited Sir Walter and Elizabeth several times, and behaved
towards them with the greatest politeness. It seemed he was
now as eager to renew the family connection as he had been
to break it off. This was very surprising. Lady Russell had a
great wish to see him and judge his character for herself.
Anne was not so enthusiastic, but she felt she would rather
see Mr Elliot again than not; this was more than she could say
for many other people in Bath.

Lady Russell left Anne at Sir Walter's rented house in
Camden Place, and went on to her own house in Rivers
Street. Anne entered the house without any hope of
enjoyment, but was pleased to find her father and sister glad
to see her. They were eager to show her the house and
furniture, and to tell her how pleasant life was in Bath. Their
house was the best in Camden Place, without a doubt, and
their social life, they told Anne, was extremely busy. They
were invited everywhere. All the best families in Bath were
anxious to have Sir Walter and his daughter at their evening
parties, their dinners, their musical evenings. Could Anne
wonder that her father and sister were happy there?

And they had Mr Elliot, too! He was not only forgiven,
they were delighted with him. He had been so ready to
apologize for the past that there was now a perfect
understanding among them all. He had even given an
explanation for his early marriage. It seemed that his wife, a
rich woman, had been wildly in love with him and
determined to marry him. She had also been a very fine-

looking woman. A very fine-looking woman, with a large fortune, desperately in love with William Elliot! Sir Walter considered it a complete apology, and even Elizabeth thought it acceptable.

Anne listened, but without quite understanding why Mr Elliot was now so interested in Sir Walter's family. She could only think that he hoped to marry Elizabeth; Elizabeth and her friend Mrs Clay certainly appeared to believe it.

Sir Walter Elliot and his daughter Elizabeth were invited everywhere.

49

The talk was of Mr Elliot for most of the evening, and Sir Walter described his appearance in some detail.

'He is not a bad-looking man; indeed, better to look at than most men. And there are very few handsome faces in Bath,' Sir Walter added. 'I was in Bond Street one morning, and counted eighty-seven women go past, one after the other, and not one pretty face among them! It was a very cold morning, to be sure, and cold air is never kind to women's faces.'

Sir Walter turned to Anne. 'How is Mary looking?' he said. 'The last time I saw her, she had a red nose, but I hope that does not happen every day.'

'Oh no, I'm sure it doesn't,' said Anne. 'Mary has been in good health, and is looking very well.'

'I was thinking of sending her a new hat, but I'm afraid that would make her want to go out in cold winds. And that would be so bad for her face.'

Anne wondered whether she could suggest that a new dress would not have that worrying effect, but at that moment there came a sudden knock on the door.

It was Mr Elliot, full of apologies for calling so late in the evening, but anxious to know if the ladies were well. There were polite words on all sides, and then Mr Elliot was introduced to Anne.

He recognized her at once as the woman whose face he had admired in Lyme, and Anne was amused by his surprise. He was extremely handsome, and his manners were so good that she could compare them only to one other person's. When he sat down to talk to them all, Anne found his conversation both sensible and interesting, and he seemed especially eager to talk to her and hear her opinions. She had never expected that her first evening in Camden Place would pass so pleasantly.

Now that she was back with her family, Anne wanted to find out, not only if Mr Elliot was in love with Elizabeth but, more importantly, if her father was in love with Mrs Clay. She found herself alone with Sir Walter the next morning.

'My dear Anne,' said the baronet at once, 'I must say how much prettier you are looking these days. I expect you are using Gowland's cream on your face?'

'No, I use nothing at all,' replied Anne, hiding a smile.

'Well, I *am* surprised! Gowland's is excellent. Mrs Clay has been using it, on my advice, for weeks now, and you can see how it has quite taken away her freckles.'

To Anne's eyes the freckles looked very much the same as before, and she wished Elizabeth had heard their father talking like this. 'Surely she would agree that Mrs Clay is a danger!' Anne thought. 'But perhaps it will not matter if my father marries again, if Elizabeth is going to marry Mr Elliot. And I will always have a home with Lady Russell.'

She decided to stop worrying about Mrs Clay, although she knew that Lady Russell was still very annoyed at Mrs Clay's continued presence in Camden Place.

Mr Elliot, however, was fast becoming a favourite with Lady Russell. She admired his manners, his understanding, his opinions, his warm heart, and his attachment to family. His past bad behaviour was now explained as the natural

Mr Elliot was without doubt a very pleasant friend to have.

mistakes of a very young man, and Lady Russell began to think it would be a very good thing if he married again. She suspected that Mr Elliot also had marriage in mind, and that his admiration was not for Elizabeth, but for someone else.

Anne was still uncertain about the reasons for Mr Elliot's new enthusiasm for friendship with her family, but he was now a frequent visitor to Camden Place, and he was without doubt a very pleasant friend to have.

They did not always agree, however. He considered social rank and connection far more important than she did. An example of this was when Lady Dalrymple and her daughter arrived in Bath. Lady Dalrymple (in Anne's opinion, most unfortunately) was a cousin of Sir Walter's, and there had been a disagreement between the families some years before. Now, however, Sir Walter and Elizabeth were desperate to be included in the Dalrymples' social circle in Bath.

The words 'our cousin, Lady Dalrymple' sounded in Anne's ears all day long, and she was ashamed that her father and sister were so painfully eager for people to know of their connection to a high-ranking lady.

But William Elliot thought it was quite natural. 'My dear cousin,' he said, 'you and I know that Lady Dalrymple and her daughter are dull people, but they move in the best social circle and so are good friends for the Elliot family to have.'

'My idea of good friends, Mr Elliot,' said Anne, 'is clever, well-informed people, who make interesting conversation.'

'No, those are not good friends,' he said gently, 'those are the best. But the connection with the Dalrymples can only be good for the name of Elliot, dear cousin, and the Elliot name is one we can all be proud of.'

'Well,' said Anne, 'I certainly am proud, too proud to enjoy a welcome that depends only on social rank.'

'I love your anger,' said Mr Elliot smiling; 'it is very natural. We are both proud, but perhaps in ways that are a little different. There is one thing, though,' he added quietly, 'that I am sure we will agree on. We should feel grateful if a new connection, like Lady Dalrymple, is useful in helping Sir Walter forget a certain person who is of lower rank than he is.'

As he spoke, he looked meaningfully towards the seat where Mrs Clay had just been sitting.

That was all the explanation Anne needed to understand his words, and although she realized that they did not have the same kind of pride, she was pleased with him for not liking Mrs Clay.

6

News of an engagement

While Sir Walter and Elizabeth were enthusiastically chasing the Dalrymple connection, Anne was spending time with an old school friend, Miss Hamilton, now Mrs Smith. Anne had been unhappy at school, full of sadness at losing the mother she had dearly loved, and Miss Hamilton had been kind to her in a way which Anne could never forget. Miss Hamilton had married a man of fortune not long after leaving school, and this was all Anne knew of her until they met again in Bath.

The twelve years since their last meeting had turned Anne from a shy girl of fifteen to a woman of twenty-seven with a quiet beauty and gentle manners. But her friend's life had not gone well. Her husband had spent money like water, and on his death, two years before, had left her a very poor widow. Added to these difficulties was a serious illness, which made her unable to walk. She lived in a very small house in a poor part of Bath, and could not even afford a servant. A nurse, Mrs Rooke, came in every day to help her for a few hours.

Anne began to visit her friend regularly, and was surprised to find how cheerful Mrs Smith was, almost all the time. She had loved her husband, and buried him. She had been used to having money, and it had gone. She had no child to bring happiness into her life, no family to help with her problems, no health to enjoy. But she only had moments of misery and loneliness. Most of the time she kept herself busy, and certainly did not want anyone's pity.

Anne had said nothing to Sir Walter and Elizabeth about Mrs Smith until one afternoon when Sir Walter received a sudden invitation from Lady Dalrymple to bring his family to dinner that evening. Anne was glad to have a reason for refusing the invitation.

'I have arranged to spend the evening with an old school friend,' she said.

Sir Walter and Elizabeth were not much interested in anything to do with Anne, but they asked enough questions to find out who the friend was. Sir Walter was shocked.

'And who is Miss Anne Elliot visiting? A Mrs Smith! A widow Mrs Smith. A poor, sickly, widow Mrs Smith. Really, Anne, you have the most extraordinary ideas! The name Smith can be found five thousand times in every city, and this person is your chosen friend, whom you prefer to your own family connections of high rank! Mrs Smith, what a name!'

Mrs Clay, who had been present while all this was said, now thought it advisable to leave the room. Anne made no reply, not wishing to be impolite to her father. But she wanted very much to remind him that Mrs Smith was not the only poor widow in Bath with no proud family name.

Anne heard the next day what a delightful evening they had all had at Lady Dalrymple's. Lady Russell had also been invited, and had spent the whole evening listening to Mr

Elliot describing Anne's intelligence, her gentleness, and her beauty. Lady Russell was now sure, not only that Mr Elliot was in love with Anne, but also that he would be the perfect husband for her.

'You could be very happy with him, Anne,' she told her young friend when they met the next morning, 'and it would be a most suitable connection.'

Anne smiled and blushed, gently shaking her head. 'Mr Elliot is a very agreeable man, and I think highly of him in many ways,' she said, 'but we would not suit each other.'

'Well, well, nothing is certain in this life. But my dear,' continued Lady Russell, 'if I could look forward to seeing you become Lady Elliot, and take your mother's place at Kellynch Hall – my dearest Anne, it would give me more happiness than is often felt at my time of life!'

Anne had to turn away in order to control her feelings. The idea of becoming Lady Elliot, as her mother had been, and of being able to call Kellynch her home for ever, was so attractive that for a moment she could say nothing. But when she imagined Mr Elliot actually proposing marriage to her, calmness returned. She could never accept him.

Although she had known him for a month now, she could not be sure that she really knew his character. She could see he had had bad habits in the past, and she did not completely trust him. She suspected him of being a clever, careful man, who always said the right thing, and was good at pleasing everybody. He was not open or honest enough for Anne, who found warm, enthusiastic people more attractive.

'You could be very happy with Mr Elliot, Anne,' said Lady Russell.

Lady Russell saw nothing in Mr Elliot to make her distrust him. To her he seemed the perfect gentleman, and her fondest wish was to see him marry her dear Anne in Kellynch church the following autumn.

Anne was always eager for news from Uppercross and Lyme, and one day in February she received a letter from Mary, brought to the house in Camden Place by a servant of Admiral Croft's.

My dear Anne,

I expect you are much too busy in Bath to worry about us in Uppercross. Nothing ever happens here. We had a very dull Christmas – not one dinner party all the holidays!

Today the Musgroves have sent the carriage to Lyme to bring back Louisa and the Harvilles. But we are not invited to dinner at the Great House until the day after tomorrow, because Mrs Musgrove is so afraid Louisa will be tired by the journey. I do not imagine she will be tired, as everyone will take such care of her, and tomorrow would be much better for me.

I have just heard by chance that the Crofts are going to Bath almost at once. It will be good for the Admiral's gout, it seems. They have not had the politeness to tell me, or ask to take anything for me. They are not good neighbours at all.

Yours, fondly. Mary

P.S. I am sorry to say that I am far from well.

Here the first part ended. There was a second sheet of paper, on which was written:

I kept my letter open, to give you news of Louisa, and I am glad I did. Mrs Croft has just sent me a note, offering to take anything to you – a very kind, friendly note – so I can make this letter as long as I like. What pleasant people the Crofts are! I do hope that Bath will do the Admiral's gout some good.

But now for Louisa. I have something to say that will astonish you. She is engaged to Captain Benwick! Did you guess there was an attachment between them? I never did. But we are all very pleased. It is not as good as her marrying Captain Wentworth, but far better than her marrying into a family like the Hayters, of course. Charles wonders what Captain Wentworth will say, but, if you remember, I never thought he felt anything for Louisa. And this is the end, you see, of Captain Benwick being an admirer of yours.

Anne was in no way prepared for this news. She had never been more surprised in her life. Captain Benwick and Louisa Musgrove! Luckily, her family were not much interested in the letter and did not have many questions to ask about it.

'How is Mary?' asked Elizabeth, and, without waiting for an answer, added, 'And what brings the Crofts to Bath?'

'They think the medicinal waters in Bath will be good for the Admiral's gout,' replied Anne.

'Gout!' cried Sir Walter. 'Poor old gentleman!'

'Do they know many people here?' asked Elizabeth.

Sir Walter answered calmly, 'I expect Admiral Croft will be best known in Bath as the tenant of Kellynch Hall. Elizabeth, may we introduce the Crofts to Lady Dalrymple?'

'Oh no, I think not, father. We must be careful not to make Lady Dalrymple ashamed of our connections. The

Crofts can find their own friends – there are plenty of strange-looking naval men in Bath!'

Soon Anne was able to go to her own room and think quietly about Mary's news. The cheerful, laughing Louisa, engaged to the quiet, serious Captain Benwick! What had made them fall in love? The answer came to her at once – it was their situation. For several weeks they had been thrown together, living in the same small family party. Louisa, just recovering from illness, had probably looked pale and interesting; Captain Benwick had a warm heart, and wanted somebody to love.

Anne saw no reason why they should not be happy. She hoped very much that Captain Benwick and Captain Wentworth would still be friends. And when she thought of Frederick Wentworth, free now to marry whom he chose, her heart filled with a feeling she was ashamed to recognize. Blushing, she knew it was too much like wild happiness!

One morning, about a week after the Crofts' arrival in Bath, she saw the Admiral in the street, outside a shop selling paintings of ships. He was delighted to see her, and at once asked if he could walk her home. Anne was happy to agree, and they walked along together, arm in arm.

'I expect you've heard the news, my dear,' the Admiral said with his usual openness. 'Sophy and I thought this Miss Musgrove was going to marry Frederick. But now it seems she's engaged to James Benwick.'

'A very pleasing young man,' Anne said.

'Well, ladies are the best judges. But Sophy and I cannot

help thinking Frederick's manners are better than his. However, they are certainly engaged. We heard about it from Frederick himself, by letter.'

Here was a chance for Anne to find out more. She said quickly, 'I hope, Admiral, there is nothing in the style of the Captain's letter to make you and Mrs Croft anxious about him. It did certainly seem, last autumn, that there was an

Admiral Croft and Anne walked along together, arm in arm.

attachment between him and Louisa, but I imagine that has all passed. I hope his letter shows no signs of suffering.'

'Not at all – he has too much spirit for that. No, poor Frederick must begin all over again with somebody else. No use in his going back to Uppercross, as the other Miss Musgrove, I hear, is engaged to a young man called Hayter. Sophy must get Frederick to come to Bath. There are enough pretty girls here, I am sure. Do you not agree, Miss Elliot?'

Captain Wentworth, however, was already on his way to Bath, and arrived before his sister had time to write to him. The very next time Anne left Camden Place, she saw him.

She had gone out with her sister Elizabeth and Mrs Clay. Mr Elliot was also with them, and while they were having tea in a tea-shop, it began to rain. Elizabeth noticed Lady Dalrymple's carriage across the street, and sent Mr Elliot to ask if Lady Dalrymple would kindly take them back to Camden Place.

Mr Elliot soon returned, saying that Lady Dalrymple would be delighted, but there was only room in the carriage for two. Naturally, Elizabeth would take one seat, and Anne and Mrs Clay argued politely over the second seat.

'I don't mind the rain at all,' said Anne firmly, 'and I will enjoy walking home with Mr Elliot.'

At that moment Anne caught sight of Captain Wentworth outside the tea-shop. For a few moments she could not think clearly. He entered the shop with a group of his friends, and looked shocked and confused when he saw her. They spoke

'I don't mind the rain at all,' said Anne.

a few polite words to each other, but Anne could see he was not comfortable; he looked quite red.

Elizabeth saw him, but turned her back on him coldly. Mr Elliott had disappeared, sent by Elizabeth to fetch something for her from a shop, and when Lady Dalrymple's grand carriage arrived outside, Elizabeth and Mrs Clay got up to leave. There was a little delay, and a little talking, which made sure all the other customers in the shop knew that Lady Dalrymple was calling for Miss Elliot.

Captain Wentworth, watching them, turned to Anne and offered to help her into the carriage.

'It is very kind of you,' she said, 'but I am not going in the carriage. There are not enough seats. And I prefer walking.'

'It is rather wet,' he said. 'Please take my umbrella, then, if you are determined to walk.'

'Thank you again, you are very kind, but I don't think the rain will last. I am only waiting for Mr Elliot. He will be here very soon, I am sure.'

At that moment Mr Elliot hurried in, and went eagerly to Anne's side, appearing to notice no one else but her. To the Captain he seemed to be Anne's accepted companion and friend. And in another moment, he and she were walking off together, her arm under his. Anne just had time for a gentle 'Good morning to you, Captain Wentworth' as they left.

As soon as they were out of sight, the ladies in the Captain's group of friends began talking about them.

'Mr Elliot does not dislike his cousin, I think.'

'Oh no, that is clear enough.'

'One can guess what will happen there. He half lives with the family, I believe. What a very handsome man!'

Anne found it difficult to listen to her cousin as they walked home. She could only think of Captain Wentworth. She could not understand his present feelings, whether he was suffering from disappointment or not. And until she knew that, she could not be easy in her mind.

The following morning she was out with Lady Russell in the carriage, and saw Captain Wentworth some distance away. As they came closer, she turned her head away, so that he would not see her looking at him. But she was sure that Lady Russell had seen him and was watching him closely. What was her friend thinking? What would she say about him? Anne was desperate to hear.

'You will wonder,' Lady Russell said a moment later, 'what I have been looking at. I was searching for the house which has, I have been told, the handsomest window curtains in Bath. Unfortunately I cannot remember the house number, and really, there are no very attractive curtains in this street.'

Anne blushed and smiled with pity, both for her friend and herself. They were both pretending, in one way or another.

A day or two passed without anything happening. Anne, more and more anxious to know the truth about the Captain's feelings for Louisa, became impatient for the next musical evening. This had been arranged by Lady Dalrymple and was expected to be a really good one, and as Captain Wentworth was very fond of music, Anne hoped for a few minutes conversation with him there.

She had once half promised to spend that evening with Mrs Smith, and paid a hurried visit to her to explain why she had to change their arrangement to another day.

Mrs Smith was happy with the change. 'But you must tell me all about it when you do come. Who will be there?'

Anne named all the probable guests, and when she was leaving, her friend said, half serious, half smiling, 'Well, I hope you enjoy the evening. I begin to have a feeling I may not receive many more visits from you.'

Anne was surprised and confused by this, but had no time, just then, to ask Mrs Smith what she meant.

7

The truth about Mr Elliot

Sir Walter, his two daughters, and Mrs Clay arrived at the music rooms before anyone else. But soon the door opened again, and Captain Wentworth walked in alone. Anne was the nearest to him, and stepped forward to wish him a good evening. He came to stand next to her, but after talking about the weather and Bath and the musical programme for the evening, their conversation began to die. Anne was expecting him to go at every moment, but he did not; he seemed in no hurry to leave her. After a time, he gave a little smile, and said,

'I have not really seen you since our day at Lyme. I hope you have recovered from the shock of that accident. It was a terrible hour – a terrible day!' He passed his hand over his eyes, but a moment later smiled again. 'But what a fortunate result Louisa's fall has had!'

'I certainly hope she and Captain Benwick will be happy,' answered Anne.

'Yes,' he said warmly, 'and the Musgroves have agreed to the marriage, because it is what their daughter wants. What kind parents they are! How different from—'

He stopped, perhaps remembering something that was making Anne blush. 'But I do think,' he continued, 'that

67

Louisa and Benwick are very different in character. She is a sweet girl, but James Benwick is something more – a thinking, reading man. I cannot understand how he fell in love with her. A man like him, with a broken heart! He truly loved Fanny Harville, and she was a fine, sensitive woman. A man does not – should not – ever recover from an attachment to a woman like that!'

He said no more. Anne had heard every word above the noise of talking and laughter in the room, which was now quite crowded. But before she could reply, Lady Dalrymple arrived, and Anne had to return to her own group of friends.

She did not mind, however, because her heart was now filled with happiness. She saw nothing, heard nothing of the noise in the room; she was thinking only of his words. His opinion of Louisa Musgrove . . . His surprise at Captain Benwick . . . His feelings about a first, strong attachment . . . Sentences begun, which he could not finish . . . the way he looked at her, did not look at her. All this seemed to say that his heart was returning to her at last. He must love her.

As all the guests moved into the music room, she looked around for him but could not see him. Then Mr Elliot came up to her, wanting to know the meaning of the Italian words in the first song on the programme.

She explained the meaning as well as she could. 'That is the best I can do,' she said. 'I'm afraid my Italian is very poor.'

'Yes, yes, I see it is,' said Mr Elliot. 'Very poor indeed. You have only translated all these difficult Italian song words into clear, intelligent English. You need not say anything more about your poor Italian. Here is complete proof.'

'Well, I will not argue with such kind politeness,' Anne said, 'but I would not like a real Italian speaker to hear me.'

'I know how modest you are, dear cousin,' he said, with his easy, attractive smile. 'In fact, I have been visiting in Camden Place long enough to learn all about your modesty, your beauty, your intelligence . . .'

Mr Elliot wanted to know the meaning of the Italian words.

'Too many fine words, Mr Elliot,' said Anne. 'You should be ashamed of yourself.' She looked down at the programme. 'I think the singing will begin soon.'

But Mr Elliot had not finished his fine words. 'The name of Anne Elliot,' he said, 'has an interesting sound to me. And I hope,' he added in a whisper, 'I hope that name will never change.'

Anne did not really hear these last words, because she had caught the sound of her father's voice speaking to Lady Dalrymple, just behind her.

'A good-looking man,' Sir Walter was saying. 'A very good-looking man.'

'A very fine young man indeed!' Lady Dalrymple said.

'I know his name,' added Sir Walter. 'Wentworth – a naval captain. His sister is married to my tenant, Admiral Croft, who rents Kellynch Hall.'

By now Anne had discovered the Captain, standing a short distance away. As her eyes fell on him, he seemed to turn away and did not look at her again.

Everybody began to take their seats for the singing. When Anne looked towards the Captain again, he had moved away. Anxiously, she tried to listen to the music, but the evening was long and painful to her.

Mr Elliot's last words had also made her anxious. She no longer wished to talk to him. She wished he would go away.

The first part of the programme was over. Now Anne hoped for change, for movement among the guests. She walked to the back of the room and saw Captain Wentworth not far away. He saw her too, but he looked serious and seemed undecided, and only slowly came near enough to speak to her. She felt that something must be the matter.

He spoke a few words to her. He was disappointed with the music, had expected better singing. He would not be sorry when it was over.

Anne answered in her gentle, pleasant way, with kind words for the music, but also understanding for his feelings.

The Captain replied again with almost a smile. They talked for a few minutes more; the air became warmer, more friendly. There was another smile. Perhaps he would stay to the end of the programme after all. He looked again at the programme Anne showed him, when, at that moment, a touch on Anne's shoulder made her turn round.

It was Mr Elliot. The music was about to start again. Her friends were waiting for her, and Lady Dalrymple would so much like her to explain some more Italian words. Could he offer Miss Elliot his arm to take her back to her seat?

Anne could not refuse his offered arm, but she had never found it so hard to be polite. She turned back to look at Captain Wentworth.

'I must wish you goodnight, Miss Elliot,' he said hurriedly. 'I am going – I must get home as fast as I can.'

'Is not the next song worth staying for?' asked Anne, suddenly realizing, with horror, what he was thinking.

'No!' he replied firmly. 'There is nothing worth my staying for,' and he walked quickly out of the room.

Jealousy of Mr Elliot! It was the only possible explanation.

Captain Wentworth jealous! For a moment she was all happiness. But oh! very different thoughts quickly followed. How could she take away the jealousy? How would he ever learn her real feelings?

It was misery to think of Mr Elliot's smiles and fine words. They could destroy all her hopes.

Anne could not refuse Mr Elliot's offered arm, but she had never found it so hard to be polite.

The next morning, Anne was glad that she had arranged to visit Mrs Smith. This meant she would not be at home if Mr Elliot called to see her.

Mrs Smith was eager to hear every detail of the musical evening, but Anne was ashamed to realize that she had not noticed many of the guests, or even who the singers were.

Mrs Smith was highly amused. 'You need not tell me you had a pleasant evening. I can see from your expression that last night you were with the person who interests you most in the world. You had no time to look around at other people.'

Anne blushed. In her confusion and astonishment she could find no words to say. How had her friend possibly heard about Captain Wentworth?

After a short pause, Mrs Smith continued, 'Does Mr Elliot know you are a friend of mine?'

'Mr Elliot!' repeated Anne, looking up in surprise. At once she realized her mistake and added, more calmly, 'Do you know Mr Elliot, then?'

'I did know him, in the past. We have not met for a long time. But he could be of great help to me, if you would be kind enough to ask him. You see, if *you* asked him to help me, I know it would be done.'

'I would be happy to ask him, of course,' replied Anne. 'But I suspect you think I have greater power over him than I really do have. You must think of me only as his cousin.'

Mrs Smith looked at her and smiled. 'I am sorry, my dear Anne, I have spoken too soon. But do tell me when the world will hear of your engagement to him. Next week, perhaps?'

'No,' said Anne firmly, 'nor next week, nor next, nor next. I am not going to marry Mr Elliot. I should like to know why you imagine I am.'

Mrs Smith smiled again. 'Well, well. We women never mean to accept a proposal – until it comes. And why not this one? Where could you find a more suitable husband? I am sure you hear only good about him.'

'I would never accept a proposal from Mr Elliot,' Anne said. 'He is nothing to me. It is not Mr Elliot who . . .' She stopped, blushing deeply.

There was a short silence. 'Ah,' said Mrs Smith. 'Then I think the moment has come', she continued, very seriously, 'for me to tell you all I know about your cousin. Although I believe you when you say you do not wish to marry him, perhaps in the future he will try to persuade you. So hear the truth now, and save yourself a lifetime of misery. Mr Elliot is a man without feeling or pity, a clever, cold-blooded person who thinks only of himself and destroys other people's lives. Oh! he is black at heart!'

Anne's look of astonishment made her pause, and she added more calmly, 'My words alarm you. I will tell you the facts, and you can judge for yourself. He was my dear husband's closest friend, and much poorer than we were in the early days of our marriage. My dear, generous Charles regularly lent him money, which Mr Elliot did not pay back. Much of our fortune disappeared in this way.'

'I suppose that was about the time of Mr Elliot's marriage?' said Anne.

'Oh yes, he told me all about it. His one wish was to become rich as quickly as possible, by marrying a woman with money. His wife had no social connections – her grandfather was just a shopkeeper – but he did not care about that. He told me he had only contempt for your father's rank and your sister's beauty – he just wanted money.'

'But why, then, is his behaviour towards my family so different now?'

'You have to understand that Mr Elliot's opinion about rank has changed. He has as much money as he can spend, and now he very much likes the idea of becoming a baronet – Sir William – when your father dies. So when he heard . . .'

She stopped, and listened to sounds in the next room. 'Ah, she can tell you herself. It is Mrs Rooke, the kind nurse who comes in every day.'

Mrs Smith called her in, and Mrs Rooke, a comfortable-looking woman, was only too happy to talk.

'You see, Miss Elliot, I'm also nurse to a lady called Mrs Wallis, and her husband, Colonel Wallis, is a good friend of Mr Elliot's. Mrs Wallis talks to me a lot, and she says your sister has a companion, Mrs Clay, living with her. All the servants think Mrs Clay's plan is to marry Sir Walter – they are astonished your sister is so blind to the danger. So Colonel Wallis warned Mr Elliot about Mrs Clay. That's why Mr Elliot came to Bath, to renew his connection with the family and prevent Sir Walter remarrying, if he can. He doesn't want a new little heir to take the baronetcy away from him. And now he has another reason for visiting Camden Place every day.' Mrs Rooke stopped, and looked at Mrs Smith, who continued the story.

'Yes. Mr Elliot saw you – in Lyme, wasn't it? He met you again here in Bath, as Miss Anne Elliot, and, Colonel Wallis says, is now planning to marry you.'

Here was much to think about, indeed. Mrs Rooke went back to the next room, leaving Anne and Mrs Smith alone.

'I am very glad to know all this,' said Anne. 'He is clearly a dishonest, selfish man, and now I shall know better how to behave with him. But earlier you mentioned his unkindness to you . . . What was the help that you needed from him?'

'Mr Elliot persuaded my poor husband to spend or give away all our fortune, and that is why I am so poor now. But

'Mr Elliot is now planning to marry you,' said Mrs Smith.

my husband owned a piece of land abroad, and I could live very well on the rent from this land. But there are difficulties about some payments owing, and because I have no friends to help me, and no money to pay a lawyer, I cannot do anything to solve the problem. I thought Mr Elliot would not refuse to help me, if you, as his future wife, asked him. But there is no hope of that now.'

Anne was extremely grateful to her friend for telling her the truth about Mr Elliot. Now she felt only contempt for him. She imagined her misery if she had been persuaded to marry him, and then later discovered his true character! She decided that Lady Russell must hear the truth about Mr Elliot, and Mrs Smith agreed to this.

That evening Mr Elliot came to dinner at Camden Place, and seemed a little surprised at Anne's coolly polite behaviour towards him. His smiles and smooth words had quite the opposite effect on her now, and she did not know whether to distrust him or Mrs Clay more.

The next day at breakfast she told Sir Walter and Elizabeth that she would spend the morning with Lady Russell.

'Very well,' said Elizabeth. 'Oh, and please take back that boring book she lent me, and pretend I have read it. Why will she keep lending me books? And her dress the other night at the musical evening was so ugly! I was quite ashamed of her. My best love to her, of course.'

'And mine,' added Sir Walter. 'Say I may visit her soon.'

While her father spoke, there was a knock at the door.

After the usual sounds of voices and feet on the stairs, Mary and Charles Musgrove came into the room. The surprise was very great, but Anne was really glad to see them, and even her father and sister seemed quite pleased.

They were staying in the same hotel as Mrs Musgrove, Henrietta, and Captain Harville. Mrs Musgrove had come to Bath to buy wedding clothes for Henrietta, who would soon marry Charles Hayter. There was so much news to hear, so much talking and excitement, that Anne did not have time to visit Lady Russell and tell her about Mr Elliot.

Elizabeth, after much careful thought, decided that she would have to invite everybody to Camden Place. Not a dinner . . . After all, it was only Mrs Musgrove . . . Just a small evening party . . . And they would meet Mr Elliot, and be introduced to Lady Dalrymple and her daughter.

Mary was delighted with this plan, and was the first to tell Mrs Musgrove and Henrietta about it when she, Charles, and Anne walked round to the hotel. Anne was warmly welcomed by the Musgroves, and felt very much part of the family as she heard all the news from Uppercross.

There were friends coming and going all the time in the Musgroves' hotel sitting room, and soon Captains Harville and Wentworth walked in. Anne looked towards Captain Wentworth, trying to be calm, but he did not seem to want to speak to her, and she feared that the same wrong idea about Mr Elliot was still fixed in his mind.

She continued talking to Mrs Musgrove and Henrietta about the shops in Bath, but Mr Elliot's name came up in conversation a little later, when Charles Musgrove came back in, very pleased with himself.

'Well, mother, I know you love a play, and so here are theatre tickets for tomorrow evening. Enough for all of us – Anne, Captain Harville, and you too, Captain Wentworth.'

'Oh Charles!' cried Mary. 'How can you think of such a thing? You know everybody is invited to Camden Place tomorrow night! Have you forgotten? We shall be introduced to Lady Dalrymple, and Mr Elliot will be there – Mr Elliot, our cousin, my father's heir!'

'Phoo! Phoo!' said Charles crossly. 'Don't talk to me about heirs. Who is Mr Elliot to me? What do I care for him?'

These careless words pleased Anne very much, and she saw that Captain Wentworth was now watching her closely.

The argument continued until Mrs Musgrove said, 'You had better change the tickets to another day, Charles. If there is a party at Sir Walter's, Anne will not be able to come, and I would not enjoy the play if she cannot be with us.'

Anne was very grateful for this kindness, and also for the chance to speak. She chose her words carefully.

'If it depended only on me, Mrs Musgrove, I would much rather go to the theatre with you. An evening party at home holds no interest at all for me.'

She had said it, and trembled when it was done, conscious that her words were listened to.

Captain Wentworth stood up and walked to the fireplace. A few seconds later he walked away from it and came to stand near Anne, which was probably his real plan.

'In the old days you did not like evening parties,' he said to her, 'but time makes many changes in people.'

'I have not changed so greatly!' cried Anne, and stopped, afraid of saying too much.

After a few moments he said, 'It is a long time, indeed! Eight and a half years!'

These words were still sounding in Anne's ears when she heard Henrietta calling to her, eager to go out and visit the shops. She had to move. Everybody was going out; the women one way, the gentlemen the other. There was no chance of any more conversation, and the pain for Anne of not knowing the Captain's next words was very great.

She was warmly invited to spend the whole of the next day with the Musgroves, which she promised to do, and later, she walked tiredly back to Camden Place, to spend an exhausting evening listening to Elizabeth and Mrs Clay discussing the arrangements for the party next day. Captain Wentworth had also been invited, which had both surprised and pleased Anne. For Elizabeth, it seemed, had been long enough in Bath to understand the importance of a fine naval captain. The past was nothing. The present was that Captain Wentworth would look very good, walking about her sitting room.

But would he come or not?

8

A letter for Anne Elliot

The next morning Anne was delayed by rain, and when she arrived at the Musgroves' hotel, she found Mrs Croft there, talking to Mrs Musgrove, and Captain Wentworth talking to Captain Harville. Henrietta and Mary had already gone out, and would return to collect Anne soon.

Two minutes after her arrival, Captain Wentworth said, 'I will write that letter now, Harville, if you will give me a pen and some paper.' And, turning his back on them all, he sat down to write at a separate table near the window.

Mrs Musgrove and Mrs Croft were deep in conversation, and Anne could not avoid hearing what they said.

'And so we agreed they had better marry as soon as possible,' said Mrs Musgrove in her loud whisper. 'Better than a long engagement, I told Mr Musgrove.'

'Yes, I always think a long engagement is a mistake,' agreed Mrs Croft, in her sensible way. 'So is an uncertain engagement, when the young people cannot yet afford to marry. I think all parents should prevent that if they can.'

Anne found an unexpected interest here. And at the same moment as she looked towards the distant table, Captain Wentworth's pen stopped moving. He raised his head, listening, and turned to give her one quick look.

Captain Harville now started talking to Anne, in his usual friendly way. They walked together over to the window.

'Look, Miss Elliot,' he said, showing her a small painting he was carrying, 'do you know who this is?'

'Certainly I do. It is Captain Benwick.'

'Yes, and you may guess who the picture is for. It was painted for my poor sister, and now Benwick asks me to send it back to him, to give to another woman! Wentworth is writing to him now. Poor Fanny! If she were alive, she would never forget James Benwick, as he has forgotten her!'

'No,' replied Anne, in a low, feeling voice. 'No woman who truly loved would forget the man in her life.'

Captain Harville smiled, doubtingly, and Anne, also smiling, continued, 'We certainly do not forget you men as soon as you forget us. We cannot help ourselves. We live quietly at home, so our feelings take control of us. But you always have work or some kind of business to take you out into the world, and new experiences can weaken past attachments.'

'But I believe that, as men's bodies are stronger than women's, so are our feelings.'

'Man is stronger than woman,' said Anne, 'but he does not live as long. Nor do his attachments, in my opinion. But perhaps that is a good thing for you men – you have enough difficulties and dangers in your lives. If you had a woman's feelings as well' (with a trembling voice) 'it would be too hard for you.'

'We shall never agree—' Captain Harville was beginning

to say, when they heard Captain Wentworth's pen fall to the floor; he seemed to be listening to them.

'Have you finished your letter?' asked Captain Harville.

'Not quite. I will be ready in five minutes,' he replied.

'There is no hurry. I am in good harbour here.' (Smiling at Anne) 'Well, Miss Elliot, *you* may not agree with me, but what about history, books, music? They all tell us that woman is often unfaithful.'

'Yes, but these were all written by men, who have had every advantage over us women. The pen has always been in their hands. I do not agree that books prove anything.'

'Ah!' cried Captain Harville warmly. 'If I could only make you understand what a man suffers when he says goodbye to his wife and children, and does not know if they will ever meet again! And his happiness, at the end of his voyage, when he comes into harbour and sees them waiting for him!'

'Oh yes!' cried Anne eagerly. 'I do believe you men are capable of everything great and good in your married lives. But I think that is true only while the woman you love lives, and lives for you. That is the difference – we women love longest, when the loved one is no longer there, or when all hope is gone.'

Her feelings were too strong for her to say another word.

'You are a good woman!' cried Harville, putting a kind hand on her arm. 'I cannot argue with you.'

There was movement in the room; Mrs Croft was standing up to leave. 'Frederick,' she called, 'you will be at Sir Walter's in Camden Place tonight? I know you have been invited.'

The Captain was hurriedly putting a letter together and seemed unwilling to answer fully. 'Yes, I have been invited, it's true,' he said. 'Goodbye, Sophy. Harville, are you ready? Let us go at once.'

Anne received the kindest 'Goodbye, Miss Elliot' from Captain Harville as the two men left, but from *him* not a word, nor a look. He passed out of the room without a look!

A moment later, however, the door opened again. It was Captain Wentworth. 'I am so sorry, I forgot my gloves,' he said. He crossed the room to the writing table, near where Anne was standing. With his back to Mrs Musgrove, he took out a letter from among the papers on the table, and placed it in front of Anne, looking at her with a burning question in his eyes. Then he hurriedly collected his gloves, and was out of the room again in a moment!

On the envelope was written 'To Miss A. Elliot'. While supposed to be writing only to Captain Benwick, he had also been writing to her! All that she hoped for in this world now depended on that letter! Hoping that Mrs Musgrove would not notice, she half fell into the chair where he had been sitting, and eagerly read the following words:

I can listen no longer in silence. I must speak to you in this way. I am half suffering, half hoping. Do not tell me I am too late, that love has gone for ever. I offer myself to you again, with a heart even more your own than when you almost broke it eight and a half years ago. Do not say that man forgets sooner than woman, that his love has an earlier death. I have loved none but you. Angry and unforgiving I have been, but never unfaithful. You alone have brought me to Bath. For you alone I think and plan. Have you not realized this? It is difficult for me to write, while I can hear your lovely voice. You are too good! You do believe that men are capable of true attachment. Believe me, the truest attachment is felt by

F. W.

I must go, uncertain of your reply, but I shall return as soon as possible. A word, a look will be enough to decide if I should enter your father's house tonight, or never see you again.

Anne had no time to enjoy her great happiness, because suddenly the room was full again – Charles, Mary, and Henrietta had returned from shopping. She tried to behave normally, but it was difficult to think clearly, and the others soon noticed how pale and ill she looked.

'My dear,' cried Mrs Musgrove, 'you must go home at once and rest. Charles will walk back with you.'

She and Charles left the hotel, and started walking up the street. She hoped desperately to see Captain Wentworth in the street, and to be able to say two words to him.

A moment later she heard a quicker footstep, and the Captain came up behind them. He hesitated, undecided, said nothing, only looked. He found his answer in her eyes, and the colour rose in his pale face. He walked by her side.

Then Charles said, 'Captain Wentworth, could you very kindly walk Anne home? She is rather overtired, but I have remembered an appointment I must keep.'

There could not be a difficulty with this idea. There could only be a most eager agreement, a most anxious wish to help; and hidden smiles and hearts dancing in private delight.

And so at last Anne and Frederick were able to renew the promises they had made so long ago, as they walked slowly

At last Anne and Frederick were able to renew their promises.

through the streets of Bath. Much was explained, much was remembered, talked over, and explained again.

Anne had been right. Jealousy of Mr Elliot had held him back, filled him with doubts. It was her words to Captain Harville just now that had given him hope, and made him write that letter in a great hurry.

He had loved no one but her in the eight and a half years. He had tried to forget her, and failed. He had tried, in his angry pride, to fall in love with Louisa Musgrove, and had welcomed with grateful delight his escape when she became engaged to Captain Benwick.

'I hope you will not blame Lady Russell for the past,' Anne said. 'You will learn to love her as I do, I think.'

'I will try to. Perhaps I was even more to blame than she was. When I was given my first ship to command, two years after you refused me, I did not write to renew my proposal to you. I was prevented by this stupid pride of mine! If I had asked you then, do you think you—'

'I am sure I would!' Anne cried.

'Good God! Well, eight years of separation and suffering have taught me my lesson. I must forgive other people sooner than myself, I must forget my pride, and I must value the happiness I am so fortunate to have!'

Who can be in doubt of what followed? No one tried to persuade Anne and Captain Wentworth against marriage this time. Sir Walter even thought the marriage quite a suitable one for Anne, and was happy to write the Captain's name on the correct page of his favourite book, *The Baronetage*. Lady Russell saw that she had been wrong about both Mr Elliot and the Captain, and as she loved Anne better than she loved herself, she had no difficulty in becoming very fond of Anne's husband. Mary was delighted to have a married sister, and one whose husband was richer than either Henrietta's or Louisa's husband. Elizabeth was less happy; there were no proposals of marriage for *her*, and no expectation of any in the future.

William Elliot, hearing the news of his cousin Anne's engagement, soon left Bath and returned to London. He did succeed in preventing Sir Walter from marrying Mrs Clay, because Mrs Clay also left Bath and was next heard of in London, living with Mr Elliot. And clever as Mr Elliot was, perhaps Mrs Clay was cleverer. It seemed possible that she might still become a baronet's wife one day, when Mr Elliot became Sir William Elliot.

Mrs Smith was the first visitor to Captain and Mrs Wentworth after their marriage. The Captain solved the problems with the widow's land abroad, and arranged for her to receive regular payment of the rent. She and Anne continued to be good friends.

Anne's life was now full of happiness, loved and loving in her turn. She was proud of being a sailor's wife, and only the fear of a future war could throw shadows on her sunshine.

GLOSSARY

Admiral an officer of very high rank in the navy

admire to enjoy looking at someone or something; to have a very good opinion of someone or something; **admiration** *(n)*

ancient very old

anxious worried or nervous

astonish to surprise someone very much; **astonishment** *(n)*

attachment a feeling of liking or love for a person or place

attractive pleasing; good-looking

baronet a man who has the lowest rank of title which can be passed from father to son; **baronetcy** the rank or position of a baronet

behaviour the way that someone behaves

blush *(v)* to become red in the face because you are embarrassed or ashamed

capable able to do something well

carriage a vehicle, pulled by horses, for carrying people

cheerful looking or sounding happy

compare to look at two people or things to see how similar or different they are

connection something that joins people or things together

contempt a feeling that someone or something is worthless

cottage a small, simple house, usually in the country

determined *(adj)* sure that you want to do something

duty something that you feel you have to do because it is right

eager very interested and enthusiastic about something that you want to do

elder/eldest older/oldest (used only of people, especially of members of a family)

engaged having promised to marry someone; **engagement** *(n)* an agreement to marry

firm *(adj)* strong and determined

forgive to stop feeling angry with someone who has done something to harm you or make you unhappy

freckles small brown marks on a person's skin (often on the face)

gentleman a man of good family, usually rich

gloves a covering for the hands, made of wool, leather, etc.

gout a disease that causes painful swelling, especially in the toes, knees, and fingers

Gowland's cream a face cream recommended by Sir Walter

harbour *(n)* an area of water on the coast where ships can shelter, protected from the open sea by strong walls; a safe place

hedge a line of small trees planted together

heir someone who will receive a person's money or title when that person dies

inn a hotel

manner(s) polite behaviour

mind *(n)* the part of a person that thinks and feels

modest not talking much about your own abilities

navy the part of a country's armed forces that fights at sea; **naval** *(adj)*

overturn (of a carriage) to turn on its side

pale (of a person's face) having light-coloured skin, or skin whiter than usual because of illness, fear, etc.

persuasion the act of persuading someone to do something or to believe something

pity *(n)* a sympathetic understanding of another person's troubles

power the ability to control people or things

pride being proud

propose to ask someone to marry you; **proposal (of marriage)** *(n)*

rank a certain level in society, in the army or navy, etc.

recover to get better after an illness or the death of a loved one

rent *(v)* to pay to use another person's house or land

servant a person who is paid to do housework

shock *(n & v)* an unpleasant surprise

social connected with society and the way it is organized

spirit a strong, determined character

style a particular way of doing something

suffer to feel pain or sadness; **suffering** *(n)*

tenant a person who pays rent for the use of a house to the person who owns it

trust *(v)* to feel sure that someone is good, right, honest, etc.

unfaithful (in this story) failing to be true to the person you promised to love for ever

vain too proud of your own appearance; **vanity** *(n)*

value *(v)* to admire someone's good qualities; to think that something is important

vicar a priest in the Church of England

widow a woman whose husband is dead

ACTIVITIES

Before Reading

1 Read the introduction on the first page of the book, and the back cover. What do you know now about the people in the story? Circle **Y** (Yes) or **N** (No) for each of these sentences.

  1 Sir Walter Elliot thinks about himself a lot. Y / N
  2 Anne's sister Elizabeth is married. Y / N
  3 Lady Russell wants Anne to have a safe and comfortable future. Y / N
  4 Anne is still in love with Frederick Wentworth. Y / N
  5 Wentworth is now married to somebody else. Y / N

2 Lady Russell persuaded Anne against marriage with Frederick Wentworth for three reasons. What were they, and do you think they were good reasons? Why, or why not?

3 Imagine that you have made an important decision in your life (about your studies, marriage, living in another country, etc.). Somebody then tries to persuade you not to do it. Whose advice would you listen to, or not listen to, and why?

  a) your mother
  b) your father
  c) your grandparents
  d) your husband/wife
  e) your uncle/aunt
  f) an older sister/brother
  g) a younger sister/brother
  h) a friend of your parents
  i) your teacher
  j) your best friend

While Reading

Read Chapters 1 and 2, and then answer these questions.

Who . . .

1 . . . is Mary's husband?
2 . . . is Sir Walter Elliot's heir?
3 . . . had been Lady Elliot's close friend?
4 . . . had once hoped to marry Sir Walter's heir?
5 . . . decided to move to Bath to save money?
6 . . . knew very well how to please Sir Walter?
7 . . . had stayed with his brother at Monkford?
8 . . . lived in the Great House at Uppercross?
9 . . . became tenants of Kellynch Hall?

Before you read Chapter 3, can you guess how Anne and Captain Wentworth will behave when they meet for the first time in eight years? Choose what you think will probably happen.

1 They *look / don't look* at each other.
2 Anne *blushes / remains calm.*
3 Wentworth is *polite / rude* to Anne.
4 Wentworth *talks a lot / stays silent.*
5 They *keep their distance / fall into each other's arms.*
6 They *start arguing / don't speak to each other.*

Read Chapter 3. Who said these words, and what do they tell us about that person?

1 'We are both quite in love with him already!'
2 'You won't want to leave the little boy.'
3 'Perhaps I could go for just half an hour.'
4 'I am really not well enough to look after a sick child.'
5 'Leave the boy to my care.'
6 'A little beauty, a few smiles, and I am a lost man.'
7 'She is never tired of playing the piano.'

Read Chapter 4. Choose the best question-word for these questions, and then answer them.

What / Why / Who

1 . . . did Charles Hayter stay away from Uppercross?
2 . . . did Anne feel unhappy on the walk with the Musgroves?
3 . . . did Wentworth admire about Louisa?
4 . . . was the news about Anne that Wentworth discovered?
5 . . . did Mrs Croft offer to take Anne home in the carriage?
6 . . . enjoyed listening to Anne's conversation about books?
7 . . . noticed William Elliot's admiring look at Anne?
8 . . . happened when Louisa jumped down from the wall?
9 . . . gave the most sensible advice in an emergency?

Before you read Chapter 5, can you guess what happens?

1 Will Louisa die?
2 If she gets better, will Wentworth ask her to marry him?
3 Will Anne and Benwick fall in love?
4 Will Anne receive a proposal from William Elliot?

Read Chapters 5 and 6. There is a lot of persuasion going on in these chapters. Match these halves of sentences.

1 Sir Walter and Elizabeth were persuaded to change their opinion of William Elliot . . .
2 Sir Walter persuaded himself . . .
3 William Elliot believed that the Dalrymples were good friends to have for social reasons . . .
4 Lady Russell wanted to persuade Anne . . .
5 Anne had persuaded herself there was no hope for her . . .

6 that Gowland's cream had taken away Mrs Clay's freckles.
7 until she heard about Louisa's engagement to Benwick.
8 that William Elliot would be the perfect husband for her.
9 because of his great politeness and apologies for the past.
10 but Anne was not persuaded by his arguments.

Before you read Chapters 7 and 8, what do you think will happen? Choose some of these ideas.

1 Anne agrees to marry William Elliot.
2 Wentworth is jealous of William Elliot and fights him.
3 An old friend tells Anne the truth about William Elliot.
4 Sir Walter marries Mrs Clay and starts a new family.
5 Anne marries Captain Wentworth.
6 Elizabeth persuades William Elliot to marry her.

ACTIVITIES

After Reading

1 Perhaps this is what some of the characters in the story are thinking. Which characters are they, who are they thinking about, and what has just happened in the story at this moment?

  1 'Oh, I'm not ready for this! They're outside already, I can hear them . . . Yes, he's here, he's coming in, he's looking straight at me . . . He hasn't changed at all, not at all . . .'

  2 'Nobody ever thinks about *me*, or *my* feelings! It's *my* sister-in-law who's lying there unconscious, and they expect *me* to go home and leave *my* husband here. Well, I'm certainly not agreeing to this, and I'm going to say so, now . . .'

  3 'I've seen that face before, very recently. Where was it? Yes! It was that woman at Lyme, walking by the sea with her friends. How extraordinary that *she* should be the old man's younger daughter! And what luck for me . . .'

  4 'Oh dear! That's the one man that I particularly do not wish to see in Bath. I think it would be better if I pretend I haven't seen him. Now, I wonder if this is the street with those window curtains I have heard so much about . . .'

  5 'Well, that's done. There's no hope of my getting any help now, but at least I've made sure she knows the truth about him, and will never be persuaded to marry him.'

2 **Eight years ago, Anne ended her engagement to Frederick Wentworth. Here is their conversation. Complete Anne's side of the conversation.**

WENTWORTH: Dearest Anne, you look so sad. What is it?
ANNE: _____

WENTWORTH: Can't marry me? Why not? Your father doesn't like me, but he has not forbidden our engagement.
ANNE: _____

WENTWORTH: But *why* is she so against me?
ANNE: _____

WENTWORTH: Well, that may be true at the moment, but I'm sure I'll soon have a ship to command.
ANNE: _____

WENTWORTH: You may have a duty to *listen* to her, but you don't *have* to take her advice!
ANNE: _____

WENTWORTH: She's being *too* careful, in my opinion. There's always some danger in life. Anne, Anne, be firm!
ANNE: _____

WENTWORTH: *Wrong* to marry me? Wrong to marry the man you love? Or perhaps you don't really care for me after all?
ANNE: _____

WENTWORTH: Anne, look at me. You say you love me. So, will you marry me?
ANNE: _____

WENTWORTH: In that case there's nothing more to say. I shall leave you now, and I shall not see you again. Goodbye.

3 Here are parts of two letters written by different people in the story. Who wrote them, and to whom? Choose one suitable word to fill each gap.

1 My dear sister, you will be as _____ as I was myself _____ I heard the news _____ Benwick and Louisa Musgrove's _____. She has helped his _____ heart to recover, I _____. I hope they'll be ——— together. They seem very _____ from each other. I _____ Benwick would never love _____ woman after Fanny Harville's _____. But I was clearly _____. Louisa is a very _____ girl, who, I feel _____, will be an excellent _____ for him.

2 My dear sister, you will certainly be _____ to hear that Father's _____, Mr William Elliot, is _____ in Bath. He has _____ us several times, and _____ towards us with the _____ politeness. He is an _____ man, really handsome. His _____ are those of a _____, as you would naturally _____ of an Elliot. His _____ behaviour is all explained, _____ he is now very _____ to be part of _____ family circle. Indeed, we _____ him nearly every day . . .

4 Is *Persuasion* a good title for this story? Would any of these titles be better ones? Why, or why not?

The Baronet's Daughter	Faithfulness
A Second Chance	A Lady of Good Sense
Listen to Your Heart	The Elliots of Kellynch
A Fine Sea-Captain	Three Sisters
Harbour at Last	The Bath Connection

5 **Which of these ideas are still true in today's modern world, do you think? If they are not true, how have they changed?**

1 It is unwise to marry a young man with an uncertain future.
2 A house needs a lady to take good care of it.
3 A pleasant manner can nearly always make people forget any lack of prettiness.
4 It is wrong of a man to accept the admiration of two young women at the same time.
5 A long engagement is a mistake.
6 No woman who truly loved would ever forget the man in her life.

6 **Was Anne's marriage the ending to the story you expected? Would you prefer a different ending, like one of these? Why, or why not?**

1 In the end Anne realizes that her feelings have changed, and she would prefer to marry a gentler, more forgiving man than Captain Wentworth. She refuses his proposal.

2 Wentworth, believing that Anne will marry William Elliot, does not propose, and leaves the country. Anne does not hear from him again, and never marries.

3 Anne accepts Wentworth's proposal, but her father, full of new pride from the Dalrymple connection, will not agree to the marriage. Anne still feels it is her duty to obey her father, and breaks off the engagement for the second time.

ABOUT THE AUTHOR

Jane Austen was born in 1775 at Steventon in Hampshire, in the south of England. She was the sixth of seven children; her father was a clergyman, the Reverend George Austen, a well-educated man, who encouraged Jane both in her reading and her writing. In 1801 the family moved to Bath; then, after George Austen's death, to Southampton, and finally to Chawton in Hampshire (the house where Jane lived can still be visited). She led a quiet, uneventful life, occasionally visiting London, Bath, Lyme, and her brothers' houses. She never married, though she had several admirers. One proposal of marriage she accepted, but the next day changed her mind and withdrew her acceptance. Little is known about her love affairs, as her sister Cassandra was careful to edit Jane's private letters after her death, but it seems likely that Jane experienced disappointment in love and that she refused to marry without it. However, her life was spent in a close and affectionate family circle, and she was a much-loved aunt to her many nieces and nephews. She died in Winchester in 1817, aged only forty-two.

She started writing when she was only fourteen, and by her early twenties was already working on the first versions of some of her novels. She did not write about great events, like the French Revolution or the Napoleonic Wars, both of which happened during her lifetime. She wrote about what she knew best – the daily business of social visits, romantic affairs, and matchmaking. In a letter to a niece she wrote, 'Three or four families in a country village is the very thing to work on.' And in a reply to a suggestion for the subject of her next novel, she explained that she could not write anything without 'laughing at myself or at other people'. With characteristic modesty she finished, 'No, I must keep to my own style and go on in my own way; and though I may never succeed again in that, I am convinced that I should totally fail in any other.'

Her six major novels are now classics of English literature. They are *Sense and Sensibility, Pride and Prejudice, Mansfield Park, Emma, Northanger Abbey* and *Persuasion.* Of these, *Mansfield Park, Emma* and *Persuasion* were written in the busy parlour at Chawton, in the middle of the usual family activities and interruptions. *Persuasion* (1818) was her last novel. Jane was dying of her final illness as she wrote it, and had some difficulty in finishing it. But in a letter to her niece four months before her death, she said she had 'a something ready for Publication'. Her novels were praised for their wit and style by readers of the time, and the Prince Regent (later King George IV) enjoyed them so much that he kept a complete set of her novels in each of his houses.

The novels have remained popular since they were first published, and there is a Jane Austen Society, which guards her literary reputation and her memory jealously. There have been many film and television dramatizations of all the novels.

Jane Austen is one of the greatest novelists in the English language. Her novels are comedies of manners, dealing with parties, dresses, quarrels, engagements, and marriages, but no writer has ever drawn 'such pictures of domestic life in country villages' with a sharper eye or with a more exquisite irony.

OXFORD BOOKWORMS LIBRARY

Classics • Crime & Mystery • Factfiles • Fantasy & Horror
Human Interest • Playscripts • Thriller & Adventure
True Stories • World Stories

The OXFORD BOOKWORMS LIBRARY provides enjoyable reading in English, with a wide range of classic and modern fiction, non-fiction, and plays. It includes original and adapted texts in seven carefully graded language stages, which take learners from beginner to advanced level. An overview is given on the next pages.

All Stage 1 titles are available as audio recordings, as well as over eighty other titles from Starter to Stage 6. All Starters and many titles at Stages 1 to 4 are specially recommended for younger learners. Every Bookworm is illustrated, and Starters and Factfiles have full-colour illustrations.

The OXFORD BOOKWORMS LIBRARY also offers extensive support. Each book contains an introduction to the story, notes about the author, a glossary, and activities. Additional resources include tests and worksheets, and answers for these and for the activities in the books. There is advice on running a class library, using audio recordings, and the many ways of using Oxford Bookworms in reading programmes. Resource materials are available on the website <www.oup.com/elt/bookworms>.

The *Oxford Bookworms Collection* is a series for advanced learners. It consists of volumes of short stories by well-known authors, both classic and modern. Texts are not abridged or adapted in any way, but carefully selected to be accessible to the advanced student.

You can find details and a full list of titles in the *Oxford Bookworms Library Catalogue* and *Oxford English Language Teaching Catalogues*, and on the website <www.oup.com/elt/bookworms>.

STARTER • 250 HEADWORDS

present simple – present continuous – imperative –
can/cannot, must – *going to* (future) – simple gerunds …

Her phone is ringing – but where is it?

Sally gets out of bed and looks in her bag. No phone. She looks under the bed. No phone. Then she looks behind the door. There is her phone. Sally picks up her phone and answers it. *Sally's Phone*

STAGE 1 • 400 HEADWORDS

… past simple – coordination with *and*, *but*, *or* –
subordination with *before*, *after*, *when*, *because*, *so* …

I knew him in Persia. He was a famous builder and I worked with him there. For a time I was his friend, but not for long. When he came to Paris, I came after him – I wanted to watch him. He was a very clever, very dangerous man. *The Phantom of the Opera*

STAGE 2 • 700 HEADWORDS

… present perfect – *will* (future) – *(don't) have to, must not, could* –
comparison of adjectives – simple *if* clauses – past continuous –
tag questions – *ask/tell* + infinitive …

While I was writing these words in my diary, I decided what to do. I must try to escape. I shall try to get down the wall outside. The window is high above the ground, but I have to try. I shall take some of the gold with me – if I escape, perhaps it will be helpful later. *Dracula*

... should, may – present perfect continuous – *used to* – past perfect –
causative – relative clauses – indirect statements ...

Of course, it was most important that no one should see
Colin, Mary, or Dickon entering the secret garden. So Colin
gave orders to the gardeners that they must all keep away
from that part of the garden in future. ***The Secret Garden***

... past perfect continuous – passive (simple forms) –
would conditional clauses – indirect questions –
relatives with *where/when* – gerunds after prepositions/phrases ...

I was glad. Now Hyde could not show his face to the world
again. If he did, every honest man in London would be proud
to report him to the police. ***Dr Jekyll and Mr Hyde***

... future continuous – future perfect –
passive (modals, continuous forms) –
would have conditional clauses – modals + perfect infinitive ...

If he had spoken Estella's name, I would have hit him. I was so
angry with him, and so depressed about my future, that I could
not eat the breakfast. Instead I went straight to the old house.
Great Expectations

... passive (infinitives, gerunds) – advanced modal meanings –
clauses of concession, condition

When I stepped up to the piano, I was confident. It was as if I
knew that the prodigy side of me really did exist. And when I
started to play, I was so caught up in how lovely I looked that
I didn't worry how I would sound. ***The Joy Luck Club***